IT'S OKAY TO BE WHITE

The Best of

GREG JOHNSON

Ministry of Truth
2020

CONTENTS

TEACHER: A society in which all races and cultures live together in peace and harmony is just over the horizon.

STUDENT: What's the horizon?

TEACHER: An imaginary line that always recedes as one approaches it.

EXTRA TRACK & A
TACKY BADGE

This compilation repackages twenty-four previously published essays in order to sell them to a whole new audience. This preface, as well as "The Very Idea of White Privilege" and "It's Okay to Be White," are the "extra tracks" to get completists who already bought the rest of these essays in their original anthologies to buy them all over again. But since I openly admit it, I can hardly be accused of cynicism.

Years ago, I saw Ayn Rand's former "intellectual heir" Nathaniel Branden interviewed. He was asked a question that he had heard a thousand times before. He paused as if deep in thought . . . then repeated word-for-word the same canned answer he had repeated a thousand times before. It made concrete and vivid my long-standing conviction that, whatever his genuine intellectual achievements in his early career, he was something of a charlatan. It also deepened my strong inhibition against repeating myself.

But my audience continues to grow. So every time I repeat myself, I know that there are people hearing certain ideas for the first time. Beyond that, I am an educator, not an entertainer. There are some basic principles that new people need to hear, so I *have* to repeat them. But good educators also have a bit of entertainer in them, Alan Watts being the greatest example. I don't want to bore long-time readers, much less myself, so I try to keep my expressions, examples, and anecdotes fresh.

With this collection, I arrive at the ultimate in repetition: I am not just repeating ideas and examples, but whole essays verbatim (with a few necessary tweaks and corrections). But it needs to be done, because I have now published eleven books, and many more are in the works. Beyond that, there are also countless uncollected essays, reviews, and interviews. Thus prospective readers now wonder where to begin. Now you know. Begin here.

SOURCES

All of these essays and lectures were originally published online at *Counter-Currents*. With the exceptions of the title essay and "The Very Idea of White Privilege," they were also reprinted in my various books. The first sixteen were published as *The White Nationalist Manifesto* (Counter-Currents, 2018). "Technological Utopianism & Ethnic Nationalism," "Freedom of Speech," and "Why Race is Not a Social Construct" were published in *Toward a New Nationalism* (Counter-Currents, 2019). "In Defense of Prejudice" is the title essay of *In Defense of Prejudice* (Counter-Currents, 2017). "Spend Yourself, Save the World" and In My Grandiose Moments . . ." appeared in *Truth, Justice, & a Nice White Country* (Counter-Currents, 2015).

ACKNOWLEDGEMENTS

In addition to all the people I thanked for helping me publish these articles in the first place, wish to thank Kevin Slaughter and Scott Weisswald for helping bring this book to press.

I also thank the writers, readers, commenters, and supporters who make *Counter-Currents* possible.

This book is dedicated to Sally Hull.

Budapest, March 15, 2020

INTRODUCTION TO A
BANNED BOOK

What would you do if tomorrow morning you learned that you had one week to live—seven more days, then no future? The world would go on, but you would not be in it. At first, most people would feel shock and sadness. Some would sink into despair. Some might even kill themselves straightaway, rather than wait around. But for most of us, the initial shock would wear off, and we would say our goodbyes, put our affairs in order, and then figure out what to do with the time that remained.

Obviously, there would be little point in thinking too far ahead. Some would become intensely religious, hoping somehow to prolong their existence, but most would probably turn to short-term self-gratification. Most people don't like their jobs, so they would choose not to spend five of their last seven days on Earth working, no matter who depended on them. But they could smoke, drink, eat junk food, take hard drugs, gamble, tell people off, and even commit crimes without any fear of long-term consequences. Many people might, of course, resist these temptations because they would want to be remembered well by the people they leave behind. But very few people are willing to behave in a dignified, self-restrained, or moral manner simply as an end in itself, without external incentives.

Now imagine that not just you but the whole human race receives a death sentence tomorrow. Telescopes reveal a massive asteroid on a collision course with the Earth, an asteroid many times the size of the object that scientists believe caused the extinction of the dinosaurs. If the whole human race is going to die, with nobody to carry on our values or remember us when we are gone, there is no question that there would be an immense increase in hedonistic, nihilistic, and anti-social behavior. Social order is always threatened by a criminal rabble that must be constantly policed and suppressed. So just imagine what would happen in only a few days if this population were swelled by millions of despondent nihilists—and the policemen and prison guards who keep them contained just decide not to show up to work.

Things start breaking down in the immediate present, as soon as people lose hope for the future.

What does this have to do with White Nationalism? White demographic decline is extremely advanced in the United States. Whites have gone from being about 90% of the US population in 1965 to about 60% today, and in many locations and age groups we are already a minority. Whites are projected to slip below 50% of the population around 2042. In a democracy, that inevitably means political disempowerment.

Authoritative voices declare that white demographic decline is inevitable and hail it as a triumph of racial justice. Multiculturalists try to paint a rosy picture of a rainbow-tinted future in which whites are a minority. But whites are increasingly skeptical. Leftists and non-whites are already partying like it is 2042, openly gloating about white decline and even extinction, eager to dance on the grave of white America. It is increasingly obvious that these people really hate us. If white Americans want to see what life is like as a despised minority in a majority non-white society, they need only look at South Africa today, which was also touted as a rainbow nation.

And white people are getting the message. In the present system, we have no future, and we are acting accordingly. Loss of hope for the future is what ties together a whole array of social pathologies afflicting white Americans. After rising steadily for centuries, white life expectancies are declining, something that we would only expect in times of war, famine, plague, or social collapse.

In our case, however, the collapse has been spiritual. When people lose hope for the future, it makes no sense to go to college, marry, start families, invest in one's children, create businesses, pursue careers, or think about giving something back to society. Instead, it makes sense to turn to short-term hedonism: pornography, video games, drinking, drugs, casual sex, etc. People are increasingly failing to mature, failing to launch, failing to build relationships, failing to have lives. But short-term self-indulgence can't make us happy. Thus we see soaring rates of alienation, loneliness, anti-depressant usage, drug overdoses, alcoholism, and suicide.

There is no reason to think that the results of white demographic decline in America will be different in any other white countries.

The entire political establishment in virtually every white country is committed to the policies that are driving white demographic decline: the destruction of the family and the denigration of motherhood; the promotion of hedonism and selfishness; encouraging multiculturalism, race-mixing, and race-replacement immigration; and the cult of "diversity," which is just a euphemism for replacing whites with non-whites.

If whites have no future in the current system, then we will simply have to set up a new one. That is the goal of White Nationalism. To give our people a future again, we need a new political vision and new political leadership.

Who are White Nationalists? We are white people who have decided to have a future again, and who wish to give a future to the rest of our people. We recognize that the sources of and solutions to white decline are political. We are mature enough to understand that we cannot solve these problems as individuals, but if enough of us work together, we can turn the world around.

White Nationalism is a form of white identity politics.

White identity politics, at minimum, means that whites think of ourselves as members of an ethnic group, with collective interests, and defend those interests against conflicting groups in the political realm. Currently, the most powerful political taboo in the entire white world is against white identity politics. Just as establishment parties of the Left and Right are united in their commitment to multiculturalism and identity politics for non-whites, they are equally united in their opposition to identity politics for white people.

White identity politics can, of course, exist within a multicultural, multiracial society. For instance, "white supremacism" is a political order in which whites impose their rule and standards on people of other races.

White Nationalism, however, is not white supremacism, because we seek to replace multiracial, multicultural societies with racially and culturally homogeneous[1] homelands, which we call "ethnostates." Ethnonationalism is a universal right possessed by all races and peoples. White Nationalism is ethnonationalism for whites. *White Nationalism simply means the right of all white peoples to sovereign homelands.* We recognize that some peoples might not wish to exercise this right. For others, such as small, primitive tribes, exercising it might not be possible. But if a people chooses national self-determination, nobody else has the right to stop them.

White Nationalism is often misunderstood or misrepresented as nationalism for *generic* white people as opposed to specific white ethnic groups. But there is no such thing as a generic white person. In this world, all white people belong to specific ethnic groups. Even colonial melting-pot societies like the United States do not create generic white people, but new ethnic identities: Americans, Canadians, etc. White Nationalism means self-

---

[1] That's homogenEous, not homogenous, like milk.

determination for all white peoples, not merely generic whites, just as saving the rhino means saving all the specific subspecies of rhinos, not some sort of generic rhino.

Part 1 of this collection is called "Politics." In it, I make my case for White Nationalism based on the white demographic crisis. Whites in every country have below-replacement birth rates, often combined with widespread miscegenation and immigration by more fertile non-white populations. If these trends are not halted, whites will lose control of our historic homelands and eventually simply cease to exist as a distinct race.

All the principal causes of biological extinction apply to whites today, and since these causes of extinction result from political policies, it is meaningful to speak not just of white extinction but *white genocide*. These are the topics of Chapters 2 and 3 on "White Extinction" and "White Genocide."

To stop white genocide, we need to change the policies promoting it. We must replace our leaders before they replace us. Then we must create white homelands with pro-natal policies, so that our race in all its genetic and cultural diversity can survive and flourish again. In short, we need White Nationalism. This is the topic of Chapter 4, "Ending White Genocide."

White extinction is, of course, a long-term danger. But many horrors await us in the near future if white demographic decline is not halted. This is the topic of Chapter 5, "In the Short Run."

To create or restore white ethnostates, different groups sharing the same territories must separate. This requires moving borders and people. In Chapter 6, "Restoring White Homelands," I argue that the process of racial separation—which our enemies stigmatize as "ethnic cleansing"—need not be swift, violent, or inhumane.

In Chapter 7, "The Ethnostate," I clarify the concept of ethnonationalism and envision an ethnonationalist alternative to globalization.

In Part Two, "Philosophy," I clarify a number of fundamental ideas.

Chapter 8, "Whiteness," deals with objections to the very idea of whiteness, namely that nationalists can dispense with the concept of whiteness, that thinking in terms of whiteness undermines ethnic differences, and that there is no good definition of whiteness.

Chapter 9, "Supremacism," deals with the distinction between White Nationalism and white supremacism.

Chapter 10, "What's Wrong with Diversity?," is based on a speech at the Seventh Northwest Forum in Seattle on March 24, 2018.[2] I explain why diversity is a problem for any society. Indeed, I argue that even if whites were not facing extinction, the problems with diversity still constitute a case for ethnonationalism.

The opposite of diversity is "Homogeneity," so in Chapter 11, I explain what White Nationalists mean by this term. Finally, in Chapter 12, "Whitopia," I discuss the question of utopianism: Who is guilty of utopian political fantasies, White Nationalists or multiculturalists?

In Part Three, "Activism," I describe the cultural and political movement necessary to make White Nationalism a reality. Chapter 13, "Politics, Metapolitics, & Hegemony," defines these crucial concepts and explains what victory would look like and how to get there. Chapter 14, "A Winning Ethos," lays out a few simple rules that will allow the White Nationalist movement to become maximally powerful and persuasive. In Chapter 15, "The Relevance of the Old Right," I explain why White Nationalists need to distance ourselves from National Socialism, Fascism, and similar political movements to which our enemies—and many of our friends—continually try to link us. Chapter 16, "As Inevitable as We Make It," offers reasons to feel

---

[2] I want to thank V.S. for the transcription.

optimistic about our cause.

I believe my arguments have something to offer patriots of all nations, both white and nonwhite. But the fact that I am a white American inevitably colors my outlook, particularly in Part Three. I believe that our movement needs to emphasize "metapolitics," i.e., creating the conditions necessary for political success, *wherever those conditions do not exist.* But where such conditions do exist, for instance in countries like Italy, Poland, and Hungary, the focus of ethnonationalist-populist parties should be on actually winning political power. But in the United States and the rest of the Anglosphere, as well as most of Northern and Western Europe, the metapolitical conditions are not yet right. The purpose of this collection—which is itself a work of metapolitics—is to help change that.

NOTES ON THE SUPPLEMENTAL CHAPTERS

Chapter 17, "The Very Idea of White Privilege," is printed here for the first time. It is the text of my talk for the seventh meeting of the Scandza Forum in Oslo, Norway, on November 2, 2019. I was unable to speak because the Norwegian government—without knowing the topic or even the title of my lecture—somehow determined that it would cause violence. Thus I was detained by armed police and escorted out of the country.[3]

Chapter 18, "Technological Utopianism & Ethnic Nationalism," is the text of my talk at the fourth meeting of the Scandza Forum in Copenhagen, Denmark, on September 15, 2018. In my previous Scandza Forum talk, "Redefining the Mainstream" (reprinted in *Toward a New Nationalism*) I argued that we need to craft ethnonationalist

---

[3] See Greg Johnson, "Anarcho-Tyranny in Oslo," *Counter-Currents*, November 6, 2019 and "The Norwegian Police Security Service's Order to Arrest Greg Johnson," *Counter-Currents*, November 15, 2019.

messages for all white groups, even Trekkies. This is my Epistle to the Trekkies, explaining why globalization is not compatible with progress toward technological utopianism and why ethnonationalism is the best political order to lead mankind to the stars.

In Chapter 19, "Freedom of Speech," is my talk at the third Erkenbrand Conference in the Netherlands on Saturday, November 3, 2018. I argue that freedom of speech is not just an instrumental value for ethnonationalists. It is also something that we should want to protect in our ideal states.

Chapter 20, "In Defense of Prejudice," argues that a large part of what Leftists proclaim as the sin of "prejudice" is simply how intelligent human beings classify entities into kinds and predict the future based on past experience. Leftism makes irrationality a moral imperative.

Chapter 21, "Why Race is Not a Social Construct," argues that races are natural kinds that we can directly perceive, not social constructs and criticizes the most common arguments for the idea that race is a social construct.

Chapter 22, "Spend Yourself, Save the World," and chapter 23, "In My Grandiose Moments," are inspirational and motivational pieces on the ethos of idealism and self-sacrifice necessary to make White Nationalism a reality.

Chapter 24, the title essay, is printed here for the first time. It is a tribute to, and rhapsody on, the classic meme "It's Okay to Be White," which is one of the most effective tools we have for revealing the establishment's anti-white agenda. Our enemies don't want whites to stop being arrogant, supremacist, or genocidal. They want us to cease to exist.

There was bound to be a backlash. This book is part of it, and now so are you. Welcome to the resistance.

WHITE EXTINCTION

White Nationalists believe that the current social and political system has put our race on the road to biological extinction. If present trends are not reversed, whites will disappear as a distinct race.

To many whites, this sounds like an absurd and alarmist claim, given that there are anywhere from 700 million to one billion of us on the planet today. Part of that skepticism is simply psychological denial in the face of an unpleasant prospect. Non-whites seldom show skepticism about white extinction. Indeed, our enemies take our eventual disappearance for granted and openly gloat about our decline.

I wish to argue, however, that white extinction is not an alarmist fantasy, but an alarming fact, the inevitable conclusion of sober, informed analysis.

Since my eyes glaze over when anyone resorts to mathematical models, charts, graphs, and technical jargon, I will construct my argument in the simplest possible terms. First, I will merely argue that white extinction is a *plausible* idea, not a far-fetched and fanciful one. Then I will argue that, if present trends continue, white extinction is not just possible, but *inevitable*.

In biological terms, the white race is a subspecies of the larger human species, *Homo sapiens*. When a species goes extinct, that includes all its subspecies, of course. But when a subspecies goes extinct, other subspecies of the same species might still survive. Both species and subspecies go extinct because of the exact same causes. From the point of view of conservation biologists, the extinction of a subspecies is to be fought just as adamantly as the extinction of a whole species. Indeed, a species perishes—or is saved—one subspecies at a time.

For economy of expression, I will simply speak of the extinction of species. But when I refer specifically to *white* extinction, it should be understood that I am referring to a subspecies of mankind.

Biologists claim that up to 99.9% of species that have ever existed on this planet are now extinct. Furthermore, many extinct species enjoyed dramatic advantages over whites. For instance, most extinct species existed far longer than our race before facing extinction. The average lifespan of a species is 10 million years, whereas whites have been around for only about 40,000 years.

Some extinct species also existed in far greater numbers than whites today. For instance, in 1866, a single flock of passenger pigeons was observed in southern Ontario. The flock was one mile wide, 300 miles long, and took 14 hours to pass. It is estimated to have contained 3.5 billion birds, which is 3-and-a-half to 4 times the entire white population of the world today. Less than 50 years later, however, the entire species was extinct due to hunting and habitat loss. In 1914, Martha, the world's last passenger pigeon, died in the Cincinnati Zoo. In 1875, a swarm of Rocky Mountain Locusts covered 198,000 square miles (greater than the area of California). It was estimated to contain 12.5 trillion insects. Within 30 years, the species was extinct.

Some living species have existed for a very long time. The horseshoe crab has been around for 450 million years. The coelacanth fish has existed for 400 million years. The lamprey has been around for 350 million years. The New Zealand Tuatara lizard has existed for 200 million years.

But based on natural history, we can say that *simply by virtue of existing*, there is a 99.9% chance that our race will become extinct. If we want to be among the long-term survivors, we certainly can't just depend upon luck.

Human beings—whites especially—do have an advantage over other species: our intelligence and creativity can help us to discover and defeat the causes of extinction. We are, in fact, the only species on this planet that can aspire to make itself immortal through science, technology, and wise government.

Unfortunately, our intelligence is now being used to create artificial conditions that promote white extinction. Extinctions are divided into natural (like the dinosaurs) and man-made (like the dodo and the passenger pigeon). White extinction is not natural but man-made. Thus, if our race is to survive, the first thing we must do is not defeat nature, but other men.

Extinction is not merely the death of all members of a race. After all, every living thing dies. But if all the members of a race die *without replacing themselves*, then the race becomes extinct. Thus extinction is not merely death—which comes to us all—but *failure to reproduce*. Extinction is inevitable if a race fails to reproduce itself. Extinction *just is* failure to reproduce.

For the existing white population to reproduce itself, each couple must average 2.1 children—2 children to replace themselves, and .1 to replace the race by taking up the slack of those who fail to reproduce at all. The image of a "normal" family—father, mother, and two children—is actually the happy, smiling face of creeping racial annihilation, for if sub-replacement fertility persists long enough—if more people die than are born—our race will eventually cease to exist. If you take more money out of your account than you put in, your balance will reach zero. It is basic arithmetic.

Having a third child is the difference between contributing to the slow death of our race or to its healthy growth. Thus White Nationalists need to do everything in our power to create a new "normal" image of the three-child white family, as opposed to the one- or two-child family. Unfortunately, white birth rates as a whole and in every white country are below replacement. This means that white extinction is inevitable if current trends are not reversed.

What are the causes of reproductive failure, i.e., extinction? Biologists give four basic causes:

- ❖ *Loss of habitat*, meaning the environment necessary for sustaining and reproducing the species. Loss of habitat can take place through sudden or slow geological or climate change, the loss of food sources, etc.
- ❖ *Invasive species*, meaning competition for resources by another species in the same ecological niche.
- ❖ *Hybridization*, also known as "genetic pollution," meaning reproduction, but not reproduction of one's distinct biological type. Hybridization is only possible if a sufficiently similar species invades one's ecological niche.
- ❖ *Excessive predation*, meaning that a species is killed by predators faster than it can reproduce itself. Predation includes epidemics. Excessive predation is, in effect, genocide: the killing off of an entire group. Genocide can, however, be divided into hot and cold varieties. Hot genocide is the quick and violent extermination of a group. Cold genocide is the slow destruction of a group simply by establishing conditions that make its long-term survival impossible. Cold genocide could, therefore, also include the other causes of extinction: habitat loss, invasive species, and hybridization.

All of these causes of extinction can be natural or man-made.

Now let's examine our ongoing extinction in terms of

these four biological causes.

Habitat loss: the ongoing conquest of nature through science and technology would seem to be expanding white habitats. Man can live at the north and south poles, the bottom of the oceans, and even in space. It is conceivable that someday we will be able to transform other planets into human habitats.

But there is a sense in which white reproduction is suffering due to habitat loss: whites do not reproduce in unsafe environments, and one of the greatest causes of unsafe breeding environments is the presence of non-whites. Just as pandas do not breed well in captivity, whites do not breed well in diverse environments.

In the past, whites had high birth-rates while surrounded by non-whites. But these non-whites were enslaved or otherwise subordinate and forced to emulate white standards of behavior. So whites specifically feel unsafe around *free* and *unassimilated* non-white populations, such as we find in modern multicultural societies.

The search for safe white breeding spaces is one of the driving forces behind suburbanization and exurbanization following the collapse of white supremacy, the emancipation of indigenous non-white populations, and the flooding of white lands by non-white immigrants.

Invasive species: whites in virtually every one of our nations are now facing demographic competition from non-white immigrants. Even if non-white immigration is cut off, whites will still face demographic competition from existing non-white populations which are usually more fertile.

Hybridization: race-mixing or miscegenation is a form of reproduction, in the sense that both parties pass their genes on to the next generation. But it is simultaneously a cause of racial extinction, since it fails to reproduce the racial type. Miscegenation is inevitable if different human races are allowed to associate freely in the same environment. Thus in the past, when racial integrity was valued, there were social and legal barriers to miscegenation in multiracial societies. Those barriers have been swept away.

Today, however, people are not merely "free" to miscegenate. Miscegenation is actively encouraged by the media and educational system.[1]

Miscegenation is also being forced upon whites by inter-racial rape, which is almost always perpetrated by non-white men on white women.[2] This form of rape is also being actively promoted by cultural phenomena such as pornography and the constant promotion of non-white resentment toward whites, and by social policies that encourage non-white immigration, the integration of white and non-white populations, and failure to adequately police and punish non-white criminals.

Predation: whites are not currently being subjected to fast, hot, across-the-board genocide, but the presence of large, hostile, violent, unsegregated, and poorly-policed non-white populations contributes to white extinction by causing the murder of white children and fertile adults and by causing other whites to restrict their fertili-

---

[1] See R. Houck, "The War against Whites in Advertising," *Counter-Currents*, March 23, 2018.

[2] Interracial rape statistics are rather hard to come by. In 2007, however, Lawrence Auster published a study concluding that: "In the United States in 2005, 37,460 white females were sexually assaulted or raped by a black man, while between zero and ten black females were sexually assaulted or raped by a white man. What this means is that every day in the United States, over one hundred white women are raped or sexually assaulted by a black man" (Frontpagemag.com, May 3, 2007). The phenomenon of Muslim child "grooming"—i.e., child rape—gangs in the UK is also suggestive, for the victims are overwhelmingly white, and the perpetrators are overwhelmingly non-white.

ty because of unsafe reproductive environments.

In the case of white extinction, all of these causes are man-made. Whites suffer habitat loss, invasion, hybridization, and predation from non-whites because of social policies that have dismantled white supremacy and segregation in multiracial societies; promoted non-white immigration into formerly white societies; removed barriers to miscegenation and actively encouraged it; and promoted non-white predation against whites by tearing down barriers between the races and failing adequately to police and punish non-whites when they commit crimes.

There are also *ideological, economic,* and *technological* causes of white extinction.

Ideological causes are simply ideas—including values—that promote reproductive failure, for example: hedonism, individualism, celibacy, feminism, anti-natalism, the denigration of family life, and pervasive white demonization and white guilt.

Economic causes include rising costs of family formation. This is chiefly caused by racial integration, which is the driving force behind suburbanization and ex-urbanization, as whites seek safe spaces to raise families. Non-white immigration and offshoring industry also lower wages for whites.

Of course, white people would continue to have sex in spite of these ideological and economic factors, so they would not be serious threats to white survival were it not for a *technological* factor: the availability of cheap and reliable birth control.

Voluntary birth control is also strongly dysgenic, because it requires long-term thinking and impulse control. It is often, moreover, motivated by a sense of social and ecological responsibility. To the extent that all of these traits are heritable, voluntary birth control means that future generations will be disproportionately sired by the impulsive, stupid, and morally irresponsible. High-IQ whites and Asians have limited their fertility dramatically, to the point that the least fertile societies are in Europe and the Far East. The most fertile societies are in Africa, the population of which is expected to double within the present century. If white demographic decline is not halted, the people who care least about the Earth will be the ones to inherit it.[3]

---

[3] See Greg Johnson, "Why Environmentalists Should Have Large Families," *Counter-Currents*, February 5, 2011.

WHITE GENOCIDE

I have thus far established that white extinction is a real threat. But some White Nationalists want go one step further, arguing that our race is being *intentionally* driven to extinction, i.e., that whites are the targets of genocide. This claim too is dismissed as alarmist, even crazy. Nevertheless, I shall argue that white genocide is actually happening. There are people in positions of power who are promoting policies that they know will lead to the extinction of the white race. Unless, of course, we stop them.

To establish the white genocide thesis, we must do three things. First, we need to establish that one form of genocide is a slow process of suppressing an ethnic group, leading ultimately to extinction. Second, we need to show that white extinction is not a mysterious force of nature but the result of human choices and actions. Third, we need to show that white extinction is not just an unforeseen, unintended consequence of these policies, but rather their deliberate, intentional effect.

It seems counter-intuitive to claim that whites are the victims of genocide. Whites are not being slaughtered by the millions, which is the image that most people have of genocide. To all appearances, our race is powerful, prosperous, and populous. But defenders of the white genocide thesis point to the 1948 United Nations Convention on Prevention and Punishment of the Crime of Genocide, which in Article II defines genocide as

> ... Any of the following acts committed with intent to destroy, in whole or in part, a national, ethnical, racial or religious group, as such:
> (a) Killing members of the group;
> (b) Causing serious bodily or mental harm to

members of the group;

(c) Deliberately inflicting on the group conditions of life calculated to bring about its physical destruction in whole or in part;

(d) Imposing measures intended to prevent births within the group; . . .[1]

This definition of genocide is much broader than outright mass murder. In particular, points (c) and (d) are consistent with characterizing policies as genocidal if they destroy a group slowly, over long periods of time. So genocide comes in two forms, which we can call fast, hot genocide and slow, cold genocide. White extinction falls into the latter category.

As we have seen, the causes of white extinction are not blind forces of nature, like an asteroid colliding with the Earth. They were all created by human beings. Some of them are quite recent, like feminism encouraging young women to prefer careers over motherhood, birth control pills, legalized abortion—and overturning racial segregation, immigration restrictions, and bans on miscegenation. They were hatched in the minds of intellectuals, artists, scientists, politicians, educators, and advertisers. They were made real by changing people's beliefs and values, and by altering the laws and institutions that govern us.

But all of these things could be changed. People could be taught to value family life over selfishness, hedonism, and careerism; feminism could be discouraged; access to birth control and abortion could be restricted; laws could be changed to make family formation affordable; racial separation, immigration restriction, and economic nationalism could become policy again; miscegenation could be discouraged. Indeed, White Nationalists support just

---

[1] https://treaties.un.org/doc/Publication/UNTS/ Volume%2078/volume-78-I-1021-English.pdf

such policies to halt white extinction.

But to establish the white genocide thesis, we must show that white extinction is the *intended* result of the policies we oppose. Some causes of white extinction—hedonism, individualism, feminism, birth control, abortion—are simply products of the pursuit of individual freedom. Others, like miscegenation and the social consequences of desegregation, immigration, and globalization, are products of individual freedom combined with racial egalitarianism. So isn't it possible that white extinction is just the *unintended* consequence of individualism and racial egalitarianism?

Of course it is possible, and in many cases, it is true. The majority of people who advocate individualism and racial egalitarianism are simply unaware that these values are promoting the ongoing extinction of the white race. Our job is to inform them.

But when such people are informed, their reactions fall into several categories. Some will simply refuse to accept that white extinction is taking place. Of those who accept that white extinction is actually happening, some will wish to stop it, and others will not. Of the latter, some will simply not care, and others will actually cheer the process on.

There is, however, a difference between people who might sign on to policies promoting white genocide *after the fact* and those who might conceive and execute such policies before the fact and with full awareness of their consequences. What evidence is there that the latter group exists?

First, the burden of proof needs to be shifted. For is it really plausible that the leaders of dozens of white nations have adopted similar policies antithetical to the long-term survival of their own peoples, yet *none of them knew what they are doing*?

Yes, it is fashionable to deride politicians for thinking

only in terms of the next election. But that is not really true. Politicians are, for instance, rather far-sighted when it comes to their personal career ambitions and plans. Beyond that, our ruling elites do not consist simply of democratically-elected politicians. Moreover, the ruling elites in every form of society are noted for thinking and planning ahead. Both government intelligence agencies and private think tanks are in the business of generating long-term predictions based on current trends, and planning accordingly. Thus it is just not plausible that our leaders are unaware of white extinction. They either don't care about it, or they want it to happen.

Second, Jews are a highly influential minority in politics, the media, business, academia, and the professions. Jews are, moreover, among the principal promoters of trends conducive to white genocide, such as massive non-white immigration, racial integration, miscegenation, feminism, and sexual liberation. Jewish organizations have also led the way in demonizing all pro-white ethnic activism as "hate." If whites behaved this way toward Jews, they would rightly accuse us of promoting genocide. It is simply not plausible that *all* Jews "know not what they do" when they promote harmful policies in white countries that they would fight tooth and nail in Israel.

The third and most compelling piece of evidence for white genocide is that people actually *say* that they support it. The advocates of white genocide range from marginal cranks, like Dr. Kamau Kambon, a sometime Black Studies professor and the owner of Blacknificent Books, who declared, "We have to exterminate white people off the face of the planet"[2]—to Dr. Noel Ignatiev, a Jewish Harvard Ph.D. and the editor of the journal *Race Traitor* (subtitled *Treason to Whiteness is Loyalty to Humanity*).

---

[2] Jon Sanders, "Activist: Exterminate White People," *Carolina Journal*, October 21, 2005.

Ignatiev does not speak of "exterminating" whites but merely of "deconstructing" the "concept" of whiteness.[3] This sounds like a harmless language game until you grasp that he thinks race *just is* a social construct. When the Soviets spoke of "eliminating the kulaks as a class," that was simply a euphemism for mass murder. It would be foolish to think Ignatiev is proposing anything different.

But the most common advocates of white genocide simply promote race-mixing as a solution to racism. They tacitly agree with White Nationalists that racial diversity within the same system leads to strife, so to eliminate strife, they promote miscegenation to create a homogeneous mixed race. The most influential advocate of what I call "miscegenationalism" was European unity pioneer Count Richard Coudenhove-Kalergi, who was himself of mixed race (his father was white, his mother Japanese). In his book *Practical Idealism*, he declared:

> The man of the future will be of mixed race. Today's races and classes will gradually disappear owing to the vanishing of space, time, and prejudice. The Eurasian-Negroid race of the future, similar in its appearance to the Ancient Egyptians, will replace the diversity of peoples with a diversity of individuals.[4]

Finally, white advocates have been warning our people about the threat of demographic displacement for close to a century now. For instance, Lothrop Stoddard's *The Rising Tide of Color* was published in 1920.[5] Stoddard's argu-

---

[3] Noel Ignatiev, "Abolish the White Race," *Harvard Magazine*, September–October, 2002.

[4] "Richard Nikolaus von Coudenhove-Kalergi," Wikipedia.com.

[5] Lothrop Stoddard, *The Rising Tide of Color: The Threat Against White World Supremacy* (New York: Scribner's, 1920).

ments were well-known. Yet in 1965, when Lyndon Johnson signed the Hart-Cellar immigration reform act that opened America's borders to non-white immigration, the American establishment ignored warnings about demographic displacement and placated the public with lies that it would never happen.

Once demographic displacement could no longer be ignored, the establishment switched from denying it to hailing it as progress, while silencing and marginalizing dissenting voices, quietly refusing to enforce existing immigration controls, and blocking all attempts to impose new controls.

Obviously, the people who run America *want* white demographic displacement. They are promoting white genocide. And through some strange coincidence, the leaders of virtually every other white nation are promoting the same policies.

Why is it important to establish that white extinction is actually white genocide? It is easy to understand why people might shy away from such a truth, for it implies that whites are not just the victims of a ghastly mistake, or an impersonal sociopolitical "system," or an inhuman cosmic or historical destiny, but of knowing malice, principled enmity, and diabolical evil.

It is hard to accept that such evil exists, much less that it wills our annihilation. But if we are to save ourselves, we have to understand the forces that are arrayed against us. If our attempts to raise people's consciousness and win their allegiance will eventually come up against not just ignorance and indifference but diamond-hard malice, we need to know that. Eventually we will make all the friends that we can make, persuade all the people we can persuade, and only enemies will remain—including people who are the moral equivalents of Stalin, Mao, and Genghis Khan—enemies that cannot be converted but must simply be defeated.

ENDING WHITE GENOCIDE

Whites are an endangered race. What, then, must we do to save ourselves? The same things that are done to save any endangered species or subspecies. We must determine why whites are failing to reproduce and then counter these causes. We must protect ourselves from habitat loss, invasive species, hybridization, and predation.

In a way, it is fortunate that the causes of white extinction are man-made, because all of them are within our power to correct. There are two things that we must do.

In the short run, we need to raise white birthrates until we can put long-term solutions into place.[1] When white colonists first arrived in Virginia in 1607, we belonged to a tiny minority on this continent. But we eventually explored and settled it, in part because behind us was the demographic momentum of burgeoning populations in Europe. It would be an enormous help if whites had that kind of demographic wind in our sails again.

In the long run, however, we have to address the biological and cultural causes of white extinction.

The biological causes of white extinction—habitat loss, invasive species, hybridization, and predation—can be addressed simply by creating the equivalent of wildlife preserves for whites: territories in which whites can reproduce free of the threats of invasive species, hybridiza-

---

[1] Raising white birthrates is not a long-run solution, because the problem is not that there are too few whites but too many non-whites in our countries. From an ecological point of view, a stable population of a billion or even half-a-billion whites is not necessarily a good thing. We cannot define victory as a population race with fast-breeding non-whites until the globe is laid waste.

tion, and predation. In short, we need to create or restore homogeneously white homelands, either by moving borders or moving peoples, i.e., through racial partition and secession schemes or the removal of non-white populations.

The cultural causes of white extinction can be addressed through education and social incentives: individualism can be replaced with an ethic of racial responsibility; sex-role confusion can be eliminated by the reassertion of traditional and biological sex roles (women as mothers and nurturers, men as protectors and providers); white guilt and self-loathing can be replaced by white pride and self-assertion; affordable family formation can be a cornerstone of social policy, with special incentives for more children from people with genes for high intelligence, good health, and good moral character; the option of celibacy, as well as non-reproductive sex, could also be preserved and promoted to discourage procreation by individuals with genetic problems.

Should We Stop White Genocide?

Someone might object to beginning with the question "*How* can we save the white race?" rather than the question, "*Should* we save the white race?" Of course the advocates of white genocide think that we shouldn't. But I don't think that we can change such people's minds. Instead, we should focus on convincing the vast majority of people who already firmly believe that (1) genocide is evil, (2) the extinction of animal species and subspecies is tragic, and (3) society should be willing to impose costs and inconveniences on individuals to prevent them.

Of course a large number of people have been convinced that it would not be tragic for white people to go extinct because of the terrible things white people have done throughout history. But even if all those accusations were true, that merely means that white people are a dangerous form of animal. So are tigers, lions, and sharks. But nobody would argue that it would be just for these species to go extinct because they prey on other animals. Nobody, of course, protested when the last batches of the smallpox virus were destroyed. But does anyone seriously maintain that white people are the moral equivalent of smallpox? (A disease, incidentally, that white people wiped off the face of the planet.)

White guilt is the root cause of white self-loathing, which in extreme cases leads to feeling that it would be no great tragedy if the white race simply ceased to exist. But there are a number of serious flaws with white guilt trips.

First, as Alain de Benoist pointed out, appeals to white guilt are almost always part of a moral swindle, in which people who have not actually suffered anything demand atonement, money, and privileges from people who have not actually wronged them. These uncomfortable facts are concealed by the fact that *all* whites are collectively held responsible for the acts of *some* white people, whereas *all* non-whites claim collective aggrievement because of the suffering of *some* non-whites at white hands.

But if it is legitimate for whites to feel collective guilt for the crimes of some white people, isn't it also legitimate for whites to feel collective pride in the achievements of some white people?[2] If I am guilty for all the terrible things done by Hernán Cortés and Francisco Pizarro, why don't I get credit for all the wonderful discoveries of Isaac Newton and Louis Pasteur?[3]

This is a subversive thought, because if we start tallying

---

[2] By the same token, if non-whites are supposed to take pride in the achievements of other members of their race, shouldn't they also accept collective guilt for the crimes committed by their race?

[3] This is the argument of Michael Polignano's "White Pride and White Guilt," *Counter-Currents*, December 12, 2010.

up all the positive achievements of white people in science, technology, medicine, the arts, politics, the fight to save the natural world, etc., they rapidly outweigh all the negatives, leading us to conclude that white extinction would be a great tragedy for the planet.[4]

Furthermore, does collective guilt only apply to whites? Do only non-whites have collective grievances? Are only non-whites owed collective apologies and reparations? Are Asians collectively guilty for the Mongol invasions of Europe? Are Muslims collectively guilty for the Muslim invasions of Europe? Are whites collectively owed apologies and reparations? Does the Arab world owe reparations to Africa for their part of the slave trade? Do blacks in Africa owe reparations to blacks in the New World for their role in the slave trade? Or in this case, do they want to let bygones be bygones?

Moreover, the things that white people are supposed to feel suicidally guilty about—slavery, imperialism, colonialism, genocide, environmental destruction, etc.—are hardly unique to white people. Every other race has engaged in them. Some still engage in them today.

Furthermore, if whites have outdone the other races in any of these crimes, it has only been because they were no match for our technological, commercial, and military prowess, which are actually virtues. So when we are criticized for beating other races in the struggle for power, we are being attacked as much for our virtues as our vices.

Finally, although whites were not the only people to practice slavery, hunt animals to extinction, or devastate the natural world, we are also the race that took the lead

---

[4] Charles Murray's *Human Accomplishment: The Pursuit of Excellence in the Arts and Sciences, 800 B.C. to 1950* (New York: HarperCollins, 2003) surveys the most accomplished people in science, philosophy, and the arts. More than 80 percent turn out to be "dead white males."

in abolishing the international slave trade, saving endangered species, and protecting the environment.

Moreover, colonialism and imperialism were not entirely bad, for when we abandoned our colonial empires in Africa, slavery, tribal genocide, and environmental devastation quickly reemerged. Non-white nations like India and China are also the world's greatest polluters.

So, if you want to prevent slavery and genocide, save the white race. If you want to save all the other endangered species, save the white race first.

WHY WE CAN'T STOP SHORT OF WHITE NATIONALISM

Some people who accept that white genocide is real and believe we have a duty to stop it might regard the creation of homogeneously white homelands as unnecessary. Let's consider four such arguments.

First, some might argue that it is possible for whites to survive without homelands or political power as small relict populations within larger non-white populations. Unfortunately, historical evidence does not support this. Riccardo Orizio's *Lost White Tribes* deals with six such groups: the Dutch Burghers of Ceylon, the German slaves of Jamaica, the Confederates of Brazil, the Poles of Haiti, the Basters (or Bastards) of Reheboth, Namibia (South West Africa), and the *Blancs Matignon* of Guadeloupe in the Caribbean. In all cases, these populations were eventually lost to hybridization.[5]

Second, one might argue that white relict populations can resist hybridization by adopting highly ethnocentric attitudes and marrying only among one's group, like Jews and Hindus. The problem with this suggestion is that such policies have not worked for Jews or Hindus. Jews are a

---

[5] See Andrew Hamilton, "Journeys Among the Forgotten: Riccardo Orizio's *Lost White Tribes*," *Counter-Currents*, August 2, 2013.

highly miscegenated population. But Jewish identity can survive miscegenation, since according to Jewish law, one is a Jew not through pure Jewish descent but merely through a drop of the blood of Abraham. In the case of the Hindus, the caste system was adopted only after a great deal of mixing had already taken place.

Of course, as a White Nationalist, I think it is a good thing for whites to adopt ethnocentric attitudes and avoid all race-mixing. But those attitudes will not save us if we are reduced to small, politically powerless relict populations in a sea of non-whites. So, if we adopted such ideas today, the best way of implementing them would be through the creation of homogeneously white homelands.

Third, one might argue that white extinction will not occur because our very decline might include self-correcting mechanisms which will eventually cause our population to stabilize or rise again. Now that family formation is difficult and unnecessary, divorce is easy, and birth control and abortion are widely available, individuals who are inclined by genes and culture not to reproduce—or not to reproduce with their own kind—simply don't.

That means that the next few generations of whites will be smaller, but they will be increasingly composed of people who are predisposed to reproduce, and to reproduce with their own kind. If that is true, then after a while, white birthrates will rise again. Thus whites are not going extinct. We are merely going through an evolutionary bottleneck that will ultimately render us immune to the forces that are arrayed against us.

I believe that this argument is quite plausible, but it is not a case against pursuing White Nationalist policies.

(1) It may never happen, thus we would be fools to abandon the struggle for white homelands on the chance that evolution will do our work for us.

(2) The selection pressures it posits will not make us immune to hot genocide, so it is not an alternative to cre-

ating sovereign, homogeneously white homelands.

(3) If these selection pressures do exist, it means that people will become increasingly receptive to White Nationalist policies, and once implemented, such policies will support such selection pressures.

In short, White Nationalism and the population bottleneck theory are complementary and mutually reinforcing.

Fourth, one might argue that cutting off immigration and returning to white supremacy, segregation, and legal and cultural barriers to miscegenation would be sufficient. I grant that such policies would be improvements, but not long-term solutions.

(1) If nothing is done to address below-replacement white fertility and higher non-white fertility, whites will eventually be reduced to tiny relict populations, as in scenario one. Then we will become extinct.

(2) These policies were tried and failed. The conservative fixation on doing the same thing over and over and expecting a different result is a definition of lunacy. If these policies are tried and fail again, our race may never recover.

The hour is too late for such foolishness. When our existence as a people is at stake, we can no longer afford conservative half-measures and wishful thinking. Only White Nationalism can prevent white extinction.

IN THE SHORT RUN

If present demographic trends are not halted and reversed by White Nationalism, the white race will become
extinct. Eventually. In the long run.

But this presents a problem. It is difficult to justify
making fundamental political changes today in order to
avoid catastrophes that will only unfold in the far future.
Such a program appeals only to the small percentage of
people who have the *foresight* to think about the distant
future and the *altruism* to want to make it better, even if
they will not personally benefit.

But most people are short-sighted and selfish. They
think only of the short run and have very weak senses of
responsibility, even to their own children. Their standard
response to problems like white extinction is, "It will
never happen during my lifetime, so I don't have to worry about it."

Nevertheless, we can take heart from the fact that the
environmental movement faces the exact same problem
but has been enormously successful. Moreover, small
groups of highly idealistic and altruistic people make history all time, often by exhorting people to ignore short-
term self-interest for greater long-term goods.

Indeed, such elites might be the only ones who actually make history. After all, the short-sighted and selfish
are easily outsmarted. Long games beat short games,
even in the short run. And idealists who are willing to
sacrifice themselves have a systematic advantage over
the cowardly and the selfish, other things being equal.

But even the most idealistic movements have to find
ways to move the masses through appeals to short-term
self-interest. Fortunately, diversity will cause a great deal
of ruin in white countries before our race reaches extinction. Thus White Nationalists can appeal both to the

long-term threat of white genocide and the short-term negative consequences of increasing diversity.

Furthermore, our people don't really need to *imagine* the consequences of whites becoming a minority, because there are countless cities, towns, and regions where that has *already* happened. You don't need a time machine to visit a majority non-white future. You simply need a plane ticket to Detroit or Los Angeles or London, where the future that awaits us all has already arrived.

This makes our educational work much easier. For we can simply *show* our people the lawlessness, corruption, anti-white discrimination, alienation, collapsing public services, hellish commutes, blighted cityscapes, shrinking opportunities, and pervasive hopelessness that come with white demographic replacement.

And these are mere pockets of blight within majority-white, First World countries. To appreciate what life will be like once whites are a hated and powerless minority within a majority non-white, Third World country, we only need to look at the fates of whites in Rhodesia and South Africa.

The idea that our future will be like the white minorities of Latin America is wishful thinking, for those societies are essentially white supremacist, and if whites in Europe and North America had such attitudes, we would not be facing race replacement in the first place.

The most convincing appeal to short-run self-interest is to stress the systematic anti-white inequities built into the current system. In the game of multiculturalism, whites can only lose.

Imagine multicultural politics as a poker game. Each ethnic group has a place at the table and a certain number of chips, representing its collective wealth and power. Whites currently have the largest stack. But every group gets to play a wild card, "the race card," *except* for whites. No matter how big our initial advantage might be, if we play by those rules, we can only lose.

Another way of understanding this problem is in terms of individualism vs. collectivism. Whites can't play the race card because we are individualists. We act as individuals. We believe that we must succeed or fail by our own individual merit, not as members of a group. We also believe that we must treat everyone else as an individual, not as a member of a group. Frankly, we are simply terrified of being called "racists."

Non-whites, however, get to play by different rules. When they play the race card, that simply means that they work as teams. They demand that individualists give them a fair shake in every transaction, and individualists oblige. So if non-whites offer the best product, the best price, or the most meritorious candidate, individualists hand them the prize.

But when the situation is reversed and an individualist offers the best product, price, or candidate to a non-white, the latter will give preference to members of his own tribe wherever possible, regardless of merit, regardless even of short-term self-interest. This is because he thinks in terms of maximizing the collective power of his tribe, which to him outweighs the inconveniences of employing a less competent cousin.

Of course, the non-white tribalist will *pretend* that his decision is just meritocracy at work, because if he practiced open tribal preferences, even individualists might eventually retaliate. Non-white tribes demand that we treat them as individuals. They *pretend* to reciprocate. But while we practice individualism, they practice tribalism. In short, they are cheating us. Game theory predicts that as long as whites play as individualists while non-whites work as tribes, we will lose. But individualists are slow to catch on to the scam, *because they are blind to groups.*

The tribal strategy can also be likened to parasitism. A

parasite tribe is not part of a larger body politic. Instead, it is a distinct community that lives within the larger community, a host population which the parasite tribe victimizes to its own advantage.

As long as whites continue to play this rigged game, we will continue to lose, until we have surrendered our wealth, our power, our homelands, and any control we might have over our destiny to non-white tribes—or we kick over the table and refuse to play a game rigged against us.

But how? There are only two possible solutions.

First, we can somehow convert non-white tribalists into individualists. But this will never happen, for two reasons. (1) The present system is advantageous to tribalists, so why would they throw away a winning strategy? Why would they want to adopt a moral code that would disarm them to the same sort of exploitation by some other non-white tribe? Why would they want to be losers like us? (2) White societies gave up *even trying* to assimilate non-white immigrants when we embraced multiculturalism and open borders.

Second, whites can adopt a tribal strategy. An individualist society will inevitably collapse if it is hacked by parasite tribes. To protect themselves, individualists must think of themselves as a group, with distinct interests that clash with those of other groups that live by different codes. In those clashes, whites need to take our own side. Even if we think of white identity politics as merely a temporary expedient to restore a meritocratic, individualist form of society, we need to remove parasite tribes from our societies and prevent new ones from entering, which requires that we drop the dominant taboo against identity politics for white people.

This brings us to the problem with conservatives: They conserve nothing. In the long run, White Nationalists will have to convert people from the whole of the political spectrum, Left, Right, and center. But in the short run, our natural constituency is people on the Right, who keep voting for conservative parties. If you break voters down by race, center-Right parties in every white country are increasingly becoming the parties of indigenous whites. They are *implicit* white identitarian parties, but their leaders are absolutely opposed to being explicit about this fact, much less embracing it.

The Left has spearheaded open borders and race-replacement immigration policies, and they receive the vast majority of non-white votes. For instance, in the 2016 US Presidential election, Hillary Clinton won 88% of black votes, 69% of Asian votes, and 66% of Hispanic votes—and she was an exceptionally weak candidate. The Left is, moreover, quite open about why they are committed to creating a new, non-white majority: whites consistently vote for conservative parties; once whites are in the minority, conservative parties will become un-electable, and Left-wing values will triumph.[1] In town after town, district after district, state after state across the US, the rising tide of color is drowning conservatism, establishing a Left-wing one-party state. The same fate awaits white countries around the world, unless they halt non-white immigration.

The mainstream conservative response to this blatant plan to demographically swamp and disenfranchise their electorate is a complex mixture of delusion, cowardice, and treason.

First, mainstream conservatives will never rally to the defense of their voters, because to defend whites from non-whites would be "racism" and "white identity poli-tics." Conservatives are happy to acquiesce and even to

---

[1] Tom Whitehead, "Labour Wanted Mass Immigration to Make UK More Multicultural, Says Former Adviser," *The Tele-graph*, October 23, 2009.

pander to non-white identity politics, although they know that it overwhelmingly benefits the Left. (It is now a rather old joke in America that the one black man at a Republican Party event is the keynote speaker.) But the same conservatives are absolutely committed to maintaining the taboo against appeals to race, even though only white identity politics can save them.

Second, to escape from the charge of identity politics, conservatives insist that their goal is not *to conserve a particular people*—Americans, Germans, etc.—but rather *to promote a list of abstract values*. These values, moreover, are supposedly universally valid, which means that they should appeal equally to people of other races and nations. This leads to the absurd conclusion that if Americans were completely replaced by Mexicans, this would be a triumph of conservatism as long as the new bronze nation professed belief in "el Sueño Americano." (That's "the American Dream" to you gringos.)

It is easy to understand why the Left promotes a taboo on white identity politics: Leftists know it is the only thing that will save whites from demographic replacement. It is, however, hard to understand why the Right clings to this same taboo. I used to think that conservatives were unprincipled. But I was wrong. They will happily follow the taboo against white identity politics regardless of the costs. Unfortunately, this rule was rigged by their enemies to destroy them.

The suicidal stupidity of mainstream conservatism is an enormous opportunity for White Nationalists to appeal to the short-term self-interest of large numbers of whites.

Our message is simple: As whites become minorities in our own homelands, it will be impossible for conservative politicians to win election. Therefore, it will be impossible to implement conservative policies. Therefore, the things that conservatives love will disappear. In the

United States, that means limited constitutional government, fiscal responsibility, private enterprise, freedom of speech, freedom of religion, gun rights, etc. These values have tenuous enough footholds even in white countries and are almost non-existent in non-white countries. If we wish to preserve these values, we need white identity politics today.

White liberals have taken the lead in promoting white dispossession, thus they will be most resistant to white identity politics. But even they will come around in the end. The liberal strategy is to defeat conservatives by displacing them with non-white immigrants who will vote for the Left. Once white demographic displacement creates a permanent liberal majority, liberals believe they can ensure the final triumph of religious tolerance, women's rights, drug legalization, abortion rights, gay rights, free healthcare, funding for the arts, environmentalism, organic foods, animal rights, walkable communities, etc.

But none of these values are conspicuous in Latin America, Africa, India, or the Muslim world, which are the primary sources of race-replacement immigration. Do white liberals really think that they can dictate policy to these people forever, even after non-whites have become the majority? That is a highly dubious assumption. Indeed, it smacks of an unconscious form of white supremacism.

Why would a rising non-white majority continue to uphold the values of white liberals, who have given their societies away? Wouldn't the new majority instead hold white liberals in contempt and seek to remake formerly white nations in the image of their homelands, where white liberal values have no place? If so, then the things liberals love will also disappear along with the white majority.

A racially conscious Left is not impossible.[2] We know this because it has actually existed. For instance, in the United States, Canada, Australia, and New Zealand, Asian immigration was promoted by capitalists whereas Asian exclusion legislation was promoted by the labor movement.

The key to winning over white conservatives—and eventually white liberals as well—is convincing them that the things they value are not universal but particular to white people. We will never have either American capitalism or a Scandinavian welfare state if the people who created these systems are replaced with non-white invaders. All white politics—Right or Left—is white identity politics in the end.

---

[2] See the articles tagged "racially conscious Left" at *Counter-Currents*.

RESTORING WHITE HOMELANDS

White survival requires creating or restoring white homelands. That requires racial separation. Yet even whites who find this argument compelling think that actually creating white homelands would be impossible or immoral, for the ethnostate seems to require "ethnic cleansing." Borders must be redrawn, and tens of millions of people must pack up and move. How is any of this possible without tyranny, terror, and bloodshed?

If Europe is to be preserved, millions of African, Middle Eastern, and South or East Asian immigrants must leave, and all their descendants too. In the majority-white colonial nations of North and South America and the Antipodes, some provision should be made for the remnants of indigenous populations, and perhaps some territory should be set aside for the descendants of non-white slaves. Yet millions of recent immigrants and their families must still be repatriated.

But how is that even possible? And how can it be morally justified? Matters are not helped by the revolutionary fantasy literature of William Pierce and Harold Covington, who envision ethnic cleansing through terrorism and genocide.[1]

Thus to persuade people to actually build ethnostates, White Nationalists have to deal with four questions: Is restoring white homelands even possible? Can we live with it? Is it moral? Does it have to be terrible?

---

[1] See, for instance, William L. Pierce, writing as Andrew MacDonald, *The Turner Diaries*, second ed. (Hillsboro, W.V., National Vanguard Books, 1999) and H. A. Covington, *The Brigade* (Philadelphia: Xlibris, 2008).

Is it possible for millions of non-whites to leave white nations? The best way to answer this question is with another question: Was it possible for them to come here? If it was possible for them to come, it is possible for them to leave, with all their offspring as well. With modern technology, it has never been easier for millions of people to move. Moreover, people are more rootless than ever. The average family today moves every few years. So most non-whites are moving anyway. We just want their next move to be *outside* of our homelands. In short, there is definitely a *way* to decolonize white homelands. We just need to have the *will*.

As for the question of will, two issues are relevant. First, can we *live with* repatriating non-white populations? Can we be *comfortable* with de-colonizing our homelands? Can it become part of ordinary life? Second, there is the more specific question of whether it is *moral*.

People are forced to move all the time for economic reasons:

- ❖ Once one goes onto the job market, one must go where the jobs are.
- ❖ Once one has a job, one can be moved by one's employer.
- ❖ When one loses a job, one again has to go where the jobs are.
- ❖ When the cost of living in a particular area rises, largely due to speculation in the housing market, many people whose incomes cannot keep up are forced to move to cheaper quarters.

White people seem to sleep quite well at night knowing that millions of people are forced to move for economic reasons, which all basically boil down to private greed. So white people can learn to live with encouraging people to move for a much higher purpose: the creation of a better world in which all peoples have their own homelands.

Since most people have no problem with a system that forces people to move for economic reasons, a White Nationalist government can make those reasons work for us. We don't have to be in a hurry. The next time a non-white family has to move for economic reasons, we will just make sure that they move outside our homelands.

Beyond that, whites are already living with ethnic cleansing for political reasons. It's just that whites are the *victims* rather than the beneficiaries. For two or more generations now, whites have been subjected to mass ethnic cleansing in our homelands. Millions of whites have changed homes, schools, and jobs millions of times because of the end of racially segregated neighborhoods, schools, and businesses and the influx of millions of non-white immigrants, who have destroyed white neighborhoods, schools, and jobs, forcing white families to move elsewhere in search of "better" (i.e., whiter) places to live and work. Despite the enormous human and financial costs of this ethnic cleansing, whites have been "living with it" quite well. It seldom seems to intrude into their consciousness, much less into public expression, and hardly ever into political action and change.

So I think whites can live with themselves quite well if they imposed the same processes of demographic replacement on non-whites, and I think that non-whites could live with it too.

For decades now, whites have found a way to "live with" a system in which we, as a race, have no future. Unless the present political, economic, and cultural system is fundamentally transformed, whites will become extinct in all of our homelands, and we will be replaced by non-whites. We are being subjected to a slow, cold process of genocide. Yet we are managing to "live with it," largely because we are narcotized and distracted by individualism, careerism, consumerism, hedonism, and all-round selfishness. And we are intimidated from complaining about it, much less organizing to stop it, by political correctness.

White Nationalists must wake our people up to the fact that we have no future in the present system. That awareness will make it impossible for whites to "live with" continued subjection to genocide. Then we will change that system.

To create white homelands, we must create a system where it is the non-whites who have no future in our homelands. In this case, however, "no future" is not some sort of mafia- or military-style euphemism for genocide, since non-whites have homelands all around the world, and we will make sure they get there. And if whites can live with a system in which we have no future at all, then surely non-whites can live with a system in which their people have a future in their own homelands.

Some might object that non-whites will only have bleak futures in their homelands. Notice, however, that this objection quietly discards one of the main tenets of diversity advocates, namely that non-whites who come here enrich our societies. For if non-whites enrich our societies, why would they not enrich their own societies as well? In truth, non-whites come to white societies because *we enrich them*. We provide them better lives than they can enjoy in their homelands.

But it is also true that non-white immigrants are often superior in education, ambition, and agency to the people they leave behind. They may send money home, but their departure removes something far more important: human capital. Thus non-white societies will never be able provide their citizens a decent future as long as some of their best people can leave to colonize white countries. Non-white lands will only "develop," to whatever extent possible, once white countries stop skimming off some of their best people.

One of the beauties of nationalism is that each people is responsible for its own destiny. Because whites are facing extinction, our first obligation is to ourselves. So, although we wish all peoples well, how they fare in their own homelands is ultimately not our problem.

The simple answer to the question of whether we can "live with" repatriating non-whites is that, as a race, *we can't live without it*. But that brings us to the moral question: Is repatriation the *right* thing to do?

I have already established that under the present system, whites will become extinct, and that the only real solution is the creation of white ethnostates. Therefore, non-violent removal of non-white populations is simply a matter of self-defense in the face of a mortal threat. And we all recognize the moral right to self-defense, particularly by a people facing genocide.

White genocide has not happened in a sudden burst of violence, and it will not be solved that way either. White genocide is a process unfolding over generations. Its architects knew very well that its ultimate end is the extinction of the white race. But they were not interested in a quick paroxysm of slaughter, as emotionally satisfying as that might have been. They knew that it is difficult to mobilize people to commit mass murder, and it is risky, because the victims could fight back and perhaps win, in which case one's own people might be wiped out in retaliation.

Therefore, they conceived a slower, safer process of genocide. They knew that if anti-white demographic trends were set in motion and sustained over time—i.e., lower birthrates, collapsing families, miscegenation, non-white immigration, non-white penetration of white living spaces, etc.—the long-term result would be white extinction, and very few whites would become aware of it, much less fight back, until resistance was pretty much futile anyway.

When whites regain control over our homelands, we

need to adopt similar far-sighted policies. We need to set pro-white demographic trends in motion and sustain them. Time will take care of the rest. In the short run, we need to raise white birthrates. But, again, we will never win by out-breeding non-whites until the planet is standing room only. The problem is not too few of us, but too many of them in our homelands.

Therefore, we need to set in motion a well-planned, orderly, and non-violent process of repatriation. There is, moreover, no hurry. Our enemies planned to eliminate us over generations. We can take a few decades to set things right.

To understand how it is possible to restore white homelands in a gradual, orderly, and humane manner, we need to make some distinctions. There are non-white citizens and non-white aliens. And among the aliens, there are legal and illegal aliens.

We need to deal with the aliens first. We will begin by closing the borders to non-whites. Then non-white illegals must simply be deported. The most economical way is to get them to deport themselves by cutting off their employment and benefits.

The legal ones are here on visas. We will simply not renew their visas, and when their visas expire, we will make sure that they leave.

We will also repeal birthright citizenship, and make it retroactive. We will also send the "anchor babies" back with their mothers.

But even though non-whites will no longer enjoy the rights of citizens (civil rights) in non-white countries, we will, of course, respect their *human rights* to life, property, and due process, as we do with all foreigners. In the United States alone, such policies would rid us of tens of millions of recent immigrants within a few years.

As for non-whites who are citizens, restoring white sovereignty requires that they no longer have any political power in our societies. But they will still have human rights to life, property, due process, etc., which we will of course respect. We will also respect their rights to certain government benefits, e.g., education, welfare, old-age pensions, and the like.

We must recognize that the primary demographic threat from non-whites comes from people of child-bearing age, who should be our focus. Therefore, non-whites over the age of 50 who are productive and orderly citizens should have nothing to fear from us. They should be able to work, retire, and live out their lives with all the benefits they are due, and with full protection of their human rights.

However, a White Nationalist regime would also make family reunification work in favor of emigration, so elderly non-whites will be given every incentive to join their families in their homelands, where their pensions will probably go farther.

Non-white citizens can be divided into the law-abiding and the law-breaking. Law-breakers should be imprisoned and paroled outside of our homelands. Given that a very high percentage of blacks get in trouble with the law, this policy alone would rid us of millions over a few decades.

Law-abiding non-whites of childbearing age can also be divided into industrious and upwardly mobile populations (e.g., Jews and South and East Asians) and indolent, welfare-dependent populations (primarily blacks and mestizos). The latter population will swell mightily once we end Affirmative Action and make-work programs. It would be cheaper to give them welfare for life rather than have them gum up the system by pretending to work. A White Nationalist government could give them welfare for life, as long as they collect it in their homelands.

As for the energetic and upwardly mobile non-whites, like most modern people, they move around quite a lot. We will just make sure that their next move takes them outside our homelands. Non-white schoolchildren will be educated in the native tongues of their homelands. When they reach college age, they will be sent to college overseas, so it will be natural for them to seek employment there.

Such policies would restore white homelands within a few decades, and the process would be orderly, humane, and consistent with the human rights of all parties.

To sustain a gradual and humane process of restoring white homelands, White Nationalists must, of course, not just attain but retain political power. People will be able to vote for virtually anything, but the degradation and destruction of the white race must be off the menu.

Beyond that, we must create a constellation of interest groups that profit from repatriation (moving companies, for instance). Furthermore, industries that are harmed by the process must be co-opted, divided, and otherwise neutralized as potential sources of opposition. For instance, industries that lose profits due to loss of cheap labor should receive tariff protections, price supports, bailouts—anything, really, to shut them up.

Another important consideration is that repatriation need not be a giant government program. It merely needs to make existing government programs, private institutions, and social trends work to promote non-white emigration. Most non-whites were not brought here by government programs. They brought themselves here because of private and government incentives. When those incentives are changed, many non-whites will simply deport themselves.

Due to the nature of the modern economy, most non-whites move a great deal anyway. We will simply wait until the next move, then make sure it is to a non-white country.

Due to indolence, unemployability, and criminality, many non-whites are already told where to live by the government. The next time they fall into the system, it can simply deposit them in a non-white homeland.

Many whites are uncomfortable about resettling non-whites who have put down "roots" in our homelands. But non-whites have tens of thousands of years of roots in their homelands. Yet somehow they managed to move here. So if their roots *there* did not matter to them, why should their "roots" here matter to us? And if their shallow roots here matter to us, shouldn't our own deep roots matter that much more?

Perhaps the most brazen technique of emotional manipulation used to oppose immigration control is the claim that repatriation is bad because it "breaks up families." But immigration breaks up families too, so if breaking up families is a bad thing, immigration is a bad thing as well. We will stop breaking up non-white families by stopping immigration altogether.

It is also quite brazen that the idea of family reunification is used only to argue for chain immigration. But it can just as well be an argument for chain repatriation. If family reunification is a legitimate goal of immigration policy, then we must encourage immigrants to return to the warmth of their families back in the Old Country.

One of the most common arguments for complacency in the face of demographic decline is that the disaster will happen long after we are dead. White extinction will not happen within the lifetimes of anyone alive today, but whites will slip into minority status in many countries within the lifetimes of many of my readers. Indeed, if we look at smaller units—states, counties, towns, neighborhoods, and schools—whites are slipping into minority status every single day. But certainly for older generations, such as the Baby Boomers, the worst of what we are facing will happen long after their deaths. So even though such people often support environmentalism, wildlife conservation, historical preservation, and other causes aimed at future generations, they leave white demographic decline for future generations to worry about.

White Nationalists must, of course, combat this crass and usually highly selective form of egocentrism. But whenever we cannot change this attitude, we can make it work for us. For if some people will not worry about white demographic displacement because it will happen after their deaths, why should they worry about our plan for white demographic restoration, since it too will unfold slowly over decades and only reach fulfillment well after they are dead? If some people won't fight against the coming anti-white dystopia because they won't live to see it, then why should they fight against the terrifying burrito-free dystopia White Nationalists envision, since it will only come to pass far in the future, long after the last Boomer is laid to rest?

What if a white nation decides on a gradual, peaceful, and humane process of repatriation, but non-whites respond with violence? This would simply give us an opportunity to build a consensus for more rapid and forceful forms of repatriation. The essential problem of White Nationalism is finding a way to square the requirements of white survival with our people's highly evolved, perhaps even morbid conscientiousness. But it actually makes it easier to mobilize our people if fair and reasonable solutions are violently rejected.

Even though the restoration of white homelands may take a couple of generations, there will be immediate psychological dividends for whites once we know our race has a future again. There will be less alienation and depression—fewer losers, alcoholics, drug addicts, and suicides. More whites will form families, have children, pursue degrees, start businesses, and contribute to society. Once we restore hope for the future, our people will start living as if the ethnostate is already here. Those who fight for a better world live in it today.

THE ETHNOSTATE

White Nationalists advocate not just racially but also *ethnically* homogeneous sovereign homelands, i.e., ethnostates. Sovereignty is a principle of international law. A sovereign state controls its own territory and internal affairs. It does not have to answer to any higher political authority. Sovereign states are not allowed to meddle in the internal affairs of other sovereign states. Sovereign states, moreover, regardless of their size and power, are regarded as equal under international law.

Although peoples have been fighting to establish and preserve sovereignty throughout history, the *concept* of sovereignty is a modern one, generally regarded as being established in 1648 by the Treaty of Westphalia, which ended the Thirty Years' War between Catholics and Protestants that had devastated Central Europe.

The Treaty of Westphalia established the principle that each state would adopt the church—Catholic or Protestant—of the ruling prince, and other states had to accept this. This was a pragmatic measure to end decades of religious conflict caused by the diversity of religious confessions in the same state and the church's claims to supranational authority, which licensed interventions into the religious affairs of states.

In short, the concept of sovereignty arose out of the necessity of *ensuring the right to differ.* By making social peace more important than questions of religious truth, the emergence of the modern concept of sovereignty marked the downfall of Christendom and the rise of a new hegemonic value system, liberalism.

At first, the boundaries of sovereign states were largely determined by the dynastic politics of Europe's ruling houses. But in the late 18th century, with the revival of classical republicanism, the idea of the nation-state emerged, which held that the proper sovereign entity is a people united by language, culture, and common descent.

Strictly understood, a nation-state is the same thing as an ethnostate, since the English word *nation* derives from the Latin *natio*, which refers to a group related by common descent. But in common parlance, countries like the United Kingdom, Spain, France, Belgium, Canada, and Switzerland are referred to as nation-states, even though they are multi-ethnic, quasi-imperial societies.

The confusion is compounded by the practice of using *nation* to refer to all sovereign entities, including multiethnic ones, for instance when we talk about the United Nations, international law, or international trade—all of which deal with *states*, most of which are not nation-states.

Thus we need the ideas of the ethnostate and ethnonationalism, to emphasize ethnicity as the principle of unity of a sovereign state—even though *ethnos* is just the Greek equivalent of *natio*, which makes ethnonationalism a rather redundant term.

Ethnonationalism is contrasted with *civic nationalism*, in which the principle of unity is subjection to a common system of laws or the profession of a shared civic creed. Civic nationalism need not exist in a multiracial or multicultural society, but the primary reason that civic nationalist creeds are promulgated is to deal with the absence of organic, ethnic unity in a society.

In his book *The Ethnostate*, Wilmot Robertson offers a persuasive case for ethnonationalism.[1] Ethnonationalism preserves distinct races, subraces, and cultures and allows them to evolve without the friction, distortions,

---

[1] Wilmot Robertson, *The Ethnostate: An Unblinkered Prospectus for an Advanced Statecraft* (Cape Canaveral, Fl.: Howard Allen, 1992).

and conflicts that inevitably emerge when different races and cultures are forced to share the same territory and political system.

Ethnonationalism presupposes that racial and cultural diversity are goods worth preserving. It also presupposes that this is a universal principle. To say that racial and cultural diversity are universally valuable means, first, that if a principle is objectively true, it is true for all peoples. Second, it implies that every nation ought to perpetuate itself through time and, if necessary, force other nations to respect its vital interests. Beyond that, it also implies that each nation should respect the vital interests of other nations not simply because they are willing to fight to assert themselves, but because we value the differences of others and respect their right to differ as a matter of principle.

Ethnonationalism should be seen as a *right* not an *obligation*. It is not a moral duty that needs to be adopted by every ethnic group, regardless of circumstances. It is simply a highly pragmatic tool to decrease conflict and promote genetic and cultural diversity. But ethnonationalism is not the only solution to the problems faced by multiethnic societies. For instance, Switzerland is a harmonious multiethnic society due to its decentralized, federal political system in which its 26 cantons enjoy a great deal of autonomy.

In societies like the United States and Canada, with tiny aboriginal relict populations, the best solution is the ethnic reservation where they can govern their internal affairs. Not every tribe in the Amazon or Siberia needs full sovereignty and a seat at the United Nations.

Yet another solution is the uncontested supremacism of a dominant group, in which minorities simply acquiesce to being second-class citizens or resident aliens. Such populations would enjoy the same *human rights* as foreign travelers, but no *civil rights*, meaning that all political power would lie in the hands of the dominant people. The dominant people would not just be politically but also culturally supreme, so such a society might not be entirely *ethnically* French or English or American (meaning white American), but it could be *normatively* French or English or American, and everyone within its borders would accept the normative supremacy of the dominant culture—or leave.

But whenever a people aspires to a sovereign homeland so that it can perpetuate its genetic and cultural heritage without interference, ethnonationalists believe that it has the *right* to do so, and nobody else has the right to stand in its way.

Why should sovereignty reside in ethnostates rather than in more inclusive orders, such as the European Union or the "Imperium" envisioned by Francis Parker Yockey? Or, more grandly, the "Eurosiberia" of Jean Thiriart and Guillaume Faye?[2] Or, grander still, the union of the whole Northern Hemisphere, the "Borean Alliance" or "Septentrion" of Jean Mabire and others?[3]

The principal benefits attributed to political unification are (1) preventing whites from fighting with one another, and (2) protecting whites from other racial and civilizational power blocs like China, India, and the Muslim world. These goals are important, but I think that political unification is not needed to attain them. Beyond that, it entails serious risks of its own.

The essential feature of any scheme of political unification is the *transfer of sovereignty* from the constituent

---

[2] See Guillaume Faye, "The Geopolitics of Ethnopolitics: The New Concept of 'Eurosiberia,'" *Counter-Currents*, August 25, 2010. Also see the articles tagged Jean Thiriart at *Counter-Currents*.

[3] See Greg Johnson, "The 'Borean Alliance,'" *Counter-Currents*, June 20, 2011.

parts to the new whole. If sovereignty remains with individual states, then one does not have political unification. Instead, one has an *alliance* between states, or a *treaty organization* like NATO, or an *intergovernmental organization* like the United Nations, or an economic *customs union* like the European Common Market, or a hybrid customs union and intergovernmental organization like the European Union.

But political unification is not necessary to prevent whites from fighting with one another or to secure whites from external threats. These aims can be attained through alliances and treaties between sovereign states. A European equivalent of NATO, which provides Europe with a common defense and immigration/emigration policy and mediates conflicts between sovereign member states would be sufficient, and it would have the added value of preserving the cultural and subracial distinctness of different European groups.

The threat of non-white blocs should not be exaggerated. France, the UK, or Russia alone are militarily strong enough to prevail against anything that Africa, India, or the Muslim world can throw at us—provided, of course, that whites are again *morally* strong enough to take their own side in a fight. A simple alliance of European states would be able to deter any Chinese aggression. Thus a defensive alliance between European states would be sufficient to preserve Europe from all outside forces, whether they be armed powers or stateless masses of refugees and immigrants.

As for white fratricide: the best way to defuse white ethnic conflicts is not to combat "petty" nationalism but to take it to its logical conclusion. If different ethnic groups yoked to the same system are growing restive, then they should be allowed to go their own ways. Through moving borders and moving peoples, homogeneous ethnostates can be created, in which each self-

conscious people can speak its own language and practice its own customs free from outside interference. Such
a process could be mediated by a European treaty organization, which could ensure that the process is peaceful,
orderly, humane, and as fair as possible to all parties.

International crises are by their very nature interrup-
tions in the normal order of things, which also means
that their duration is limited, so eventually everything
goes back to normal. Military alliances are also shifting
and temporary things, but political unification aims at
permanence and is very difficult to undo.

Does it really make sense to make permanent changes
in the political order to deal with unusual and temporary
problems?

The ancient Romans appointed dictators in times of
emergency, but only for a limited time, because emer-
gencies are temporary, and a permanent dictatorship is
both unnecessary and risky. The same is true of European political unification.

But what would happen if a sovereign European state
signed a treaty to host a gigantic Chinese military base?
Or if it fell into the hands of plutocrats who started importing cheap non-white labor? Clearly such policies
would endanger all of Europe, therefore it is not just the
business of whatever rogue state adopts those policies.
What could the rest of Europe do to stop this? Isn't this
why we need a politically unified Europe?

The answer, of course, is what all sovereign states do
when they face existential conflicts of interest: diplomatic pressure, economic sanctions, and, if those fail, war.
Other states would be perfectly justified in declaring war
against the rogue state, deposing the offending regime,
and removing non-Europeans from its territory. Then
they would set up a new sovereign regime and go home.

The idea that we need European unification to prevent such wars is absurd. Again, it makes no sense to

make permanent changes to solve temporary problems, and it makes no sense to, in effect, declare war on all sovereign states today because we might have to declare war on one of them tomorrow.

Political unification is not only unnecessary, it is dangerous, simply because if it fails, it would fail catastrophically. It is not wise to put all one's eggs in one basket, or to grow only one crop, or to breed a "homogeneous European man," for when the basket breaks, or blight strikes the potato crop, or a new pandemic like the Spanish flu breaks out, one is liable to lose everything.

A politically unified Europe would necessarily be ruled by a small, polyglot elite that is remote from and unresponsive to the provinces and their "petty" concerns, which they would take great pride in denigrating in the name of the greater good. If that elite became infected by an anti-European memetic virus—or corrupted by alien elites—it would have the power to destroy Europe, and since there would be no sovereign states to say no, nothing short of a revolution could stop them.

Indeed, the leadership of the present-day European Union is infected by just such a memetic virus, and it is doing all it can to flood Europe with non-whites. The only thing stopping them is the fact that the European Union does *not* have sovereign power, and stubborn sovereign ethnostates like Poland, Hungary, the Czech Republic, and Slovakia are saying no.

Even if a European Union were the only way to stop another Europe-wide war, the terrible truth is that, despite all the losses, Europe managed to recover from two World Wars. But it would not recover from replacement-level immigration promoted by a sovereign European Union.

Moreover, at a certain point, the EU is going to face a choice. If Poland or Hungary vetoes non-white immigration once and for all, the EU will either have to accept its dissolution or use coercion to hold itself together. In short, the EU may very well *cause* rather than prevent the next European "brothers' war."

A politically unified Europe would eliminate the principle of the equality of sovereign nations under international law. But it would not eliminate the existence of nations. And in a common market and political system, certain national groups—principally the Germans—would have systematic advantages and end up on top. This means that a unified Europe would end up being a *de facto* German empire, since Germany has the largest population and the strongest economy. Does anyone really think that the French or the Poles would relish living under the hegemony of priggish self-loathing German technocrats like Angela Merkel? This too is a recipe for hatred and violence, not love and harmony.

Finally, if Right-wing proponents of European unification hold that it is not really a problem for Greeks and Swedes, Poles and Portuguese to live under a single sovereign state, on what grounds, exactly, are they complaining about multiculturalism and diversity? If the EU can encompass the differences between the Irish and the Greeks, why can't it encompass the differences between Greeks and Turks, or Greeks and Syrians, etc.?

The ethnonationalist vision is of a Europe—and a worldwide European diaspora—of a hundred flags, in which every self-conscious nation has at least one sovereign homeland, each of which will strive for the highest degree of homogeneity, allowing the greatest diversity of cultures, languages, dialects, and institutions to flourish. Wherever a citizen turns, he will encounter his own flesh and blood, people who speak his language, people whose minds he can understand. Social life will be warm and welcoming, not alienating and unsettling as in multicultural societies. Because citizens will have a strong sense of identity, they will know the difference between their own people and foreigners. Because they will control their own borders and destinies, they can afford to be hospitable to diplomats, businessmen, tourists, students, and even a few expatriates, who will behave like grateful guests. These ethnostates will be good neighbors to one another, because they have good fences between them and homes to return to when commerce with outsiders becomes tiring.

The citizens of these states will be deeply steeped in their mother tongues and local cultures, but they will also be educated in the broader tradition of European high culture. They will all strive for fluency in at least one other European language. They will appreciate that all Europeans have common roots, common enemies, and a common destiny. But these commonalities are, and will remain, secondary and remote compared to linguistic and cultural differences.

The leadership caste of each ethnostate will be selected to be both deeply rooted in its own homeland but also to have the broadest possible sense of European solidarity. This ethos will allow political cooperation between all European peoples through intergovernmental and treaty organizations, as well as *ad hoc* alliances. And, since scientific truth and technological achievements are universally valid, there should be pan-European cooperation in promoting science, technology, national defense, ecological initiatives, and space exploration.

Is ethnonationalism for everyone? Yes and no.

On the one hand, we believe that all peoples have the *right* to their own homogeneous sovereign homelands, *wherever that is possible*. We want ethnostates for ourselves, and on the Lockean principle that we will take what we need for ourselves but leave other people the option of doing the same, we wish all peoples well and will honor the ethnonationalist principle wherever it is asserted, even when it might be more convenient to just boss people around and take their resources.

On the other hand, we recognize that not all peoples have an equal capacity for self-government. Successful ethnostates are certainly possible in East Asia, where today Japan and South Korea are among the most homogeneous and advanced societies on the planet. But ethnonationalism is not really possible in the racially mixed societies of Latin America, where the best option is probably a more benevolent version of the present system of rule by European-descended elites. Nor is ethnonationalism possible among the most primitive tribal peoples of the world in Africa, Amazonia, Micronesia, or Papua. Such peoples require benevolent paternalism and ethnic reservations.

But this talk of preserving the existence and distinctness of primitive peoples around the world is somewhat grandiose and premature, given that it is our existence, not theirs, that is threatened by the present global dispensation. When an airplane cabin loses pressure, you are supposed to secure your own oxygen mask before helping others. For if you die by putting the needs of others first, the people who depend on you will die as well. Once White Nationalists secure preserves for our own race, then we can benevolently entertain similar arrangements for other peoples.

WHITENESS

An obvious line of attack against White Nationalism is the claim that the very concept of whiteness is problematic. We will deal with four such objections. First, the concept of whiteness is supposed to be politically unnecessary. Second, whiteness is alleged to be subversive of ethnic identity. Third, whiteness is said to be a social construct, not a real natural kind. Fourth, the viability of White Nationalism is said to depend on an airtight definition of whiteness, which is elusive.

IS WHITENESS NECESSARY?

A common misunderstanding or misrepresentation of White Nationalism is to claim that the very concept is meaningless, because white people are not interested in "white" nationalism. We are interested in American or French or German or Italian nationalism. On this account, German nationalism is for Germans and White Nationalism is for generic white people. But there are no generic white people, so White Nationalism is a political program without a constituency, a concept without a referent.

But White Nationalism is not nationalism for generic white people. *White Nationalism just means ethnonationalism for all specific white peoples.* White Nationalists wish to preserve, restore, or create sovereign racially and ethnically homogeneous homelands for all white peoples who aspire to self-determination.

There really is no such thing as a generic white person. All white people belong to specific ethnic groups. Even in borderline cases, where the children of couples from different ethnic groups are brought up with two cultures, and even two mother tongues, we are still talking about blends of specific ethnic groups.

What differentiates white ethnic groups? There are subracial differences among Europeans, and some nations have well-defined "typical" subracial types, for instance, typical Norwegians and Finns. But other nations encompass a range of subracial types, for instance England and Italy. In short, some white ethnic groups are more biologically homogeneous than others. Thus what is essential in differentiating white nations are their distinct languages, cultures, and histories.

Since people typically marry within their faith, religious boundaries can beget ethnic boundaries. Even peoples who are genetically very similar and speak the same language—the English and the Irish, or the Serbs, Bosnians, and Croats—can be deeply divided by religion.

It is often said that White Nationalism makes sense only in colonial melting pots like the United States and Canada, in which different European ethnic groups have blended together. This is untrue. The blending of Old-World nations did not produce generic white people. It produced new ethnic groups: Americans, Canadians, Quebecois, Australians, Afrikaners, etc.

If Americans and Canadians were just generic white people, there would be no differences between them. But there are differences, and these differences are linguistic and cultural. Thus from a White Nationalist point of view, there is really no difference between European and colonial nations. We stand for the self-determination of all white nations, all over the world, not just in Europe.

Since there are no generic white people—at least outside Plato's world of forms or wherever else one finds universals—why speak of "white" nationalism at all? Why not just speak of specific national groups and be done with it?

There are five compelling reasons why we cannot avoid talking about the white race.

First, let's say we decide to avoid talk of whiteness and

instead speak only of promoting the national interests of the French, Germans, Americans, Poles, etc., while studiously avoiding any discussion of such nations as Turkey, India, or China. One has to ask: What does the first list have in common, and why are the other countries left out? The answer to both questions is that we are concerned with white nations, as opposed to non-white ones.

One might try to dodge this accusation of "racism" by speaking of "Western civilization" or "Christendom," but not all European peoples are "Western," and vast numbers of Christians are non-whites.

Basically, all attempts to avoid the word "white" are just *euphemisms*—ways of *talking around* sensitive topics, like sex or excrement, born from a fear of violating cultural taboos about polite speech. But people who can only speak of race in euphemisms are not yet ready for the struggle. It is noble to wish to save white people, but how can one muster the courage to save the white race if one can't even bring oneself to utter the word "white"? In order to battle the forces promoting white genocide, we are going to have to be more than a bit impolite.

Second, if the only motive for white skittishness about speaking in terms of race is a cultural taboo against white "racism," we need to understand the origins and functions of this taboo.

All the other races can, of course, speak in terms of racial identity and interests. And to my knowledge, Black Nationalists who speak of black power and black interests are never met with the argument, "But Black Nationalism is meaningless, because there are no generic black people, just various black tribes and nations."

Furthermore, when non-whites—or self-loathing whites —lecture us about "white privilege" and recite endless litanies of white crimes, nobody ever says, "Your accusations are meaningless. There is no such thing as a generic white person." It seems that whiteness is a completely unproblematic category when people wish to impute blame to us. It is only problematic when whites want to defend ourselves: when we wish to affirm our identity, take pride in our achievements, take stock of our interests, and take our own side in ethnic conflicts.

This taboo against any self-assertive appeal to whiteness is blatantly unfair, and whites can only lose if we continue to honor it. Obviously, this taboo was devised to systematically disadvantage whites. Thus we would be fools to continue honoring it.

Third, even though there is more to being American or English or Swedish than simply being white, we still have to talk about whiteness, because the present political system insists that it is possible for people of all races to be American or English or Swedish. For a very long time, it went without saying that only white people could be part of any European nation. But multiculturalism and civic nationalism seek to divorce European national identities from whiteness.

Thus to save our nations—and through them our race as a whole—we have to talk *explicitly* about whiteness.

We have to assert that being white is a *necessary* condition of belonging to any European national group, although of course we acknowledge that a shared language, culture, and history are also necessary.

We must assert that non-whites can be members of white nations only by virtue of legal fictions. Not every white man is a Swede, but every Swede is a white man.

Fourth, simple ethnic nationalism is not always sufficient to ensure either narrow national or broader racial interests. It is perfectly natural, normal, and right for individuals and nations to take care of their own people first. And when multiethnic empires or multinational bodies like the European Union work against the ethnic interests of specific peoples, then the "petty" nationalism of Scotland or Hungary or Poland is entirely legitimate.[1] But when petty ethnic nationalism or imperialism lead to wars between European nations, or prevent coordinated European responses to common threats, then a broader sense of pan-European racial solidarity becomes necessary to secure racial survival and flourishing.

Creating such solidarity is imperative. Thus we must emphasize *all* the things that Europeans have in common, and beyond all the differences of language, culture, and religion, the deepest root of European identity and solidarity is *racial*. All Europeans share common ancestors. We are one extended family. In order to ensure our common destiny, we need to overcome silly taboos about acknowledging and drawing strength from our common racial origins.

Fifth, colonial societies from the start involved racial distinctions between European colonists and indigenous non-whites. In some cases, African slaves and South- and East-Asian coolies were added to the mix. In such an environment, it is natural for whites not to see different nations and tribes (Aztec, Mayan), but simply different racial groupings (Indians, blacks, etc.), and it is equally natural for non-whites to see Europeans of different national origins simply as whites. Indeed, in the colonial context of racial polarization and struggle, when whites must present a unified front, the remnants of Old-World ethnic differences are actually harmful to white interests.

But now that Europe itself is being colonized by non-whites, the same process of racial polarization is taking place there as well. Blacks, Arabs, and South Asians in Europe do not see Frenchmen, Englishmen, and Germans. They simply see white men. And we simply see

---

[1] Greg Johnson, "'Let's Call the Whole Thing Off': In Defense of 'Petty' Nationalism," in *Truth, Justice, & a Nice White Country* (San Francisco: Counter-Currents, 2015).

non-whites. Our differences do not matter to them, and
their differences do not matter to us. As racial tensions
increase in Europe, our people will realize that they are
not being attacked as Frenchmen or Germans, but simply
as white men. And when Europeans resist ethnic displacement, they will increasingly regard their race as
their nation and their skin as their uniform. The sooner
we see ourselves as white people, united by common enemies and challenges, sharing a common origin and a
common destiny, the sooner we will be equal to the tasks
facing us.

IS WHITENESS SUBVERSIVE?

The best critique of whiteness as a political category
comes from Martin Heidegger. Heidegger was a support-
er of German ethnic nationalism and thought that the
National Socialist emphasis on racial whiteness subvert-
ed German ethnic interests. Heidegger understood that
whiteness is a necessary condition of being German, but
there is more to being German than just being white.[2]

Heidegger believed that making whiteness a political
concept, and subsuming Germans and other European
peoples under it, laid the groundwork for the destruction
of ethnic differences. For if we are all white, what would
it matter if Germans decided to assimilate members of
other European ethnic groups? Putting different ethnic
groups under the broad biological genus "white" leads
one to think that white people are equivalent and inter-
changeable. In biological terms, this fungibility means
that whites of other nations are *suitable breeding stock*.
And in cultural terms, fungible means *assimilable*: capable of losing one cultural identity and adopting another
one. There's also a dimension of pure power politics

---

[2] See Greg Johnson, "Heidegger and Ethnic Nationalism,"
Counter-Currents, June 27 and July 5, 2017.

here. Why would Germans biologically and culturally assimilate Poles rather than vice-versa? Obviously, simply because Germans were politically dominant.

Furthermore, the Nazis were not just interested in assimilating other whites but specifically *Nordic* whites, regardless of their culture. A corollary of this is that the Nazis would not be particularly interested in perpetuating the bloodlines of genuine Germans who were not Nordic. This consideration certainly supports Heidegger's critique, although there is no evidence that it occurred to him. But given that Heidegger himself was no Nordic *Übermensch*, it probably crossed his mind.

Heidegger's argument makes a great deal of sense. One does not even ask questions like "Are Finns white?" or "Are Italians white?" unless one is thinking in terms of breeding with them or imposing one's culture upon them. Such questions almost always arise in a colonial or imperial context. In a Europe of autonomous ethnostates, they would hardly arise at all, and only among the most rootless and cosmopolitan segments of society: academics, artists, businessmen, and the like who travel abroad and might fall in love with a foreign girl and wonder if she is "white enough" to bring back home. (One would hope that in European ethnostates, rootedness would be emphasized to those who aspire to political power.)

Fortunately, there are steps we can take to reduce the threat of European racial and cultural homogenization. We generally wouldn't need to worry about whether other peoples are "white enough" if every people has a homeland, if immigration and intermarriage between white societies are kept to a minimum, and every person has a strong enough sense of his own ethnic identity to marry his own kind. These are all sensible policies to preserve the ethnic and subracial diversity of white peoples.

Just as I am an ethnonationalist on the condition that

it is qualified by a broader white racial solidarity, I am also a White Nationalist on the condition that it preserves rather than undermines distinct white ethnic groups.

IS WHITENESS A SOCIAL CONSTRUCT?

White Nationalists are often met with the objection that race is merely a social construct, not a real biological category. In my essay, "Why Race is Not a Social Construct," I argue that this claim is false.[3] Basically, all social constructivist arguments ignore the distinction between *races*, which are objective biological facts, and *thoughts about race*—for example, racial taxonomies and scientific theories—which are socially constructed.

Here I wish to argue that whether the social construction of race is true or false, it does not pose an impediment to White Nationalism. It is simply irrelevant. We can still be White Nationalists even if race is a social construct. In fact, in some ways, it is easier.

First, one has to note that some of the very same people who treat the social construction of race as an objection to White Nationalism have absolutely no problem with advocating non-white identity politics. So if social constructivism undermines identity politics, perhaps our opponents should begin by abandoning their own. And if social constructivism is no impediment to non-white identity politics, it is no impediment to white identity politics either.

Second, White Nationalists think that identity is more than just a matter of race. Every Italian is a white man, but not every white man is Italian. Italian identity is a matter not just of common biological descent, but of a shared language, culture, and history, which are human

---

[3] Greg Johnson, "Why Race is Not a Social Construct," in *Toward a New Nationalism.*

constructs. These constructs are limited and shaped by our genetic heritage and objective historical events, but at the core of every culture are conventions which are free creations of the human imagination.

Social constructivists hold that if a group of people *think* of themselves as a nation, they *are* a nation. For White Nationalists, nationhood is *largely* a social construct, but not exclusively, since a nation also involves common descent. Nations do, of course, establish conventions for outsiders to become "naturalized" (a very revealing term), but there has always been a strong presumption in favor of making naturalization contingent on biological and cultural assimilability.

But for the sake of argument, let's just grant the social constructivist thesis that identity is entirely conventional. That does nothing to stop a society from *adopting the social convention that only white people can be members.* If social boundaries are essentially arbitrary constructs, *why not* be ethnonationalists? For a social constructivist, nothing prevents a society from stipulating racial homogeneity. And since racial diversity—regardless of whether it is real or socially constructed—is a proven source of disunity and conflict, there are sound practical reasons to prefer homogeneity.

White Nationalists believe that our race is real. But mere race realism hardly matters if people don't *think* of themselves in racial terms. White Nationalism is not just a scientific thesis. It is a political ideology. As such, it depends upon white *consciousness*, namely white *self-consciousness*. Indeed, white self-consciousness is the *greater part* of White Nationalism, for without it, whites are as politically inert as dogs or horses. Thus one of the primary activities of White Nationalists is raising white self-consciousness. Our people need to *think* that we are a distinct race, with a distinct identity and interests, which often conflict with the identity and interests of other races. And when such conflicts exist, whites must think it natural, normal, and right to organize to protect our interests in the political realm.

The social constructivists wish to knock the biological prop from under White Nationalism. But *removing race realism still leaves the greater part of White Nationalism, namely white racial consciousness, in place.* And again, if social constructivism is true, there is nothing to stop White Nationalists from simply stipulating that we want racial and ethnic homogeneity.

The only thing that would stop us from enforcing such preferences is lack of political power. Thus if social constructivism is true, White Nationalists need not waste our breath convincing every last person that our societies should be homogeneous. As long as we can sufficiently raise white self-consciousness, pride, and self-assertiveness, we can attain the political and cultural power necessary to impose our preferences on the rest of society. There is no moral reason not to do so. Our enemies openly declare their intention to do the very same thing to us.

DO WE NEED A DEFINITION OF WHITENESS?

White Nationalism does require an answer to the question: "Who are whites?" But it does not require an airtight *definition* of whiteness. There is an important distinction between a phenomenon and its definition. The white race is a phenomenon that exists in the real world. Our primary acquaintance with white people is through sense perception. We know whites when we see them.

Definitions are attempts to verbally articulate the essential traits of what we see in sense perception, and since we can always perceive more than we can say, all definitions are inadequate. But the lack of a good definition does not imply that we don't *know* who white people are, much less that white people don't *exist*. It simply proves that when confronted with the richness of nature, words fail us again and again.

Most of us would be hard-pressed to give a verbal definition of cabbage that would allow us to distinguish it from lettuce. But we can instantly tell them apart simply by looking at them. We always know more than we can say. Thus it is pure sophistry to argue that if we can't offer an airtight definition of cabbage, then we don't know what cabbages are, let alone that they don't even exist.

For the purposes of White Nationalism, white people are the aboriginal peoples of Europe and their unmixed descendants around the world. But inevitably White Nationalists are challenged to defend any such account of whiteness against certain borderline cases.

- ❖ How much non-white blood is consistent with being a white person?
- ❖ Are Jews, Persians, Georgians, and Armenians white or non-white? Some clearly look white, others not.
- ❖ Are Balkan Muslims white or non-white?[4]

Again, these questions don't really matter in a world where all peoples have their own homelands. Jews might not be "white enough" for your taste, but they are all Jewish enough to live in Israel.

Of course, non-white nationalists are never met with the same challenge, and they wouldn't be deterred if they were.

The underlying assumption of these objections is that if one cannot provide *non-arbitrary* rules for dealing with borderline cases, then whiteness is a social construct, not

---

[4] The answer is that they are white people whose religion is a vector of non-white invasion into Europe. Sadly, we can now say the same about most European Christians as well.

a natural kind. But this is as absurd as arguing that, since there are shades on the color spectrum that straddle blue and green, pure instances of blue and green do not exist. There have been many different racial taxonomies, which divide up the races of the world in different ways.[5] But none of these taxonomies fail to include a category for white people, because white people obviously exist.

But again, let's just grant the social constructivists their point. If we embrace social constructivism, we are completely free to answer these questions with arbitrary rules of thumb. Social constructivists should be the *last* people to object to the idea of white nations being empowered to define their identities and determine who is in and who is out.

Finally, most demands to "define white" are offered in bad faith. The very people who claim that White Nationalism fails without an airtight definition of whiteness, have no problem singling us out when they wish to blame us for the world's problems, discriminate against us in education and employment, or target us for genocide. So when one of these people asks you to define whiteness, smile and tell him that white people are the ones who are supposed to feel white guilt. But if whites are real enough to bear white guilt, then we are real enough to build white nations.

---

[5] See Andrew Hamilton, "Taxonomic Approaches to Race," *The Occidental Quarterly*, vol. 8, no. 3 (Fall 2008).

SUPREMACISM

The charge that White Nationalists are "white supremacists" has two aspects. First, there is the claim that whites think of ourselves as superior to other groups. Second, there is the idea that whites want to rule over other groups.

I do think that whites are superior to some groups in some ways. I am very proud of our people, and we have a great deal to be proud of. In the areas in which we excel, we have done a lot for the world. Our superior achievements in comparison to other races are why so many non-whites are flooding into white societies. There's no need to mince words about that or apologize in any way.

It is easy to find ways in which we are superior to other groups. But we can also find ways in which we are inferior to other groups. I just don't think this issue matters, however, because as Kevin MacDonald and Jared Taylor have pointed out, even if we were the sorriest lot of people on the planet and had accomplished almost nothing, it would still be natural, normal, and right for us to love our own and to be concerned with the future of our people. And it would still be politically expedient to demand our own sovereign homelands.

As for the idea of whites reigning over other people, I don't want that. I am a universal ethnonationalist. I believe in self-determination for all peoples. The people who are actually committed to whites ruling over other people are civic nationalists who claim to be Western civilizational chauvinists but not ethnic or racial nationalists. Civic nationalists have basically conceded multiracialism to the Left. It is a victory they are not even going to question, much less try to roll back.

Chauvinism is an attitude of superiority. A Western

chauvinist believes that Western civilization is superior. What is Western civilization, though? Basically, it is white civilization. Thus civic nationalists are committed to the idea of white civilizational superiority, which is the first form of supremacism. They try to evade this implication with a hat trick, of course, declaring that Western civilization is a *universal* civilization, but this is simply false.

Western civilization is a product of white people, and the people who are most comfortable in Western countries are white people. When blacks, Asians, and other groups come to white countries, they want to change things to suit them better. The Western chauvinist must say "no." Non-whites have to live by white standards, including white laws, which are of course enforced by the state. In effect, this means whites must rule over non-whites. This is white supremacism in the second sense.

Now I certainly believe that if non-whites live in white societies, we absolutely must impose our values on them, or they will create a society that we do not want to live in.

We really need to reflect for a moment on the absurdity of the situation in which it is now "problematic" for white values to be "supreme" in white societies, which were created and sustained by white people and white values. Does anyone denounce Japan for being Asian supremacist or Nigeria for being black supremacist?

But we have to be honest that it really is a form of oppression to impose white standards on non-white populations and demand that they "assimilate," that they surrender their identities, that they in effect go around wearing clothes that don't fit. Because one's civilization should be as comfortable and as becoming as a well-tailored suit.

Blacks, for instance, don't find white civilization comfortable. It is like demanding they wear shoes that are two sizes too small when we impose our standards of punctuality and time preferences, demand that they follow our age-of-consent laws, or foist the nuclear family upon them. These things don't come naturally to Africans. Imposing such standards is the hated "white supremacy" system. But if we don't impose white standards upon blacks, we have chaos. We have great cities like Detroit transformed into wastelands.

William Blake once said, "One law for the lion and ox is oppression." Because lions and oxen are different beasts, to put them under one law forces them to live contrary to their natures. White supremacism would be like lion supremacism: demanding that the ox live by the code of the lion. But the ox doesn't eat meat. He eats grass. Eating meat doesn't come naturally to him. The true white supremacists are the civic nationalists, who would think they are doing the ox a favor by declaring meat the "universal" diet and force-feeding it to him.

White Nationalists are not white supremacists, because it is not our preference to rule over other groups. Although if *forced* to live under multicultural systems, we are going to take our own side and try to make sure that our values reign supreme, our preference is to go our separate ways. That's reason enough for an amicable, no-fault racial divorce, so we can live in the manners that most befit us in our own separate homelands.[1]

---

[1] See Greg Johnson, "Irreconcilable Differences: The Case for Racial Divorce," in *Truth, Justice, & a Nice White Country*.

WHAT'S WRONG WITH DIVERSITY?

There are contexts in which diversity is a good thing. For instance, diversity of goods in the marketplace, diversity of options in life, diversity of opinions in politics and academia, and a diversity of points of view on juries for awarding prizes or deciding court cases.

But in the context of contemporary politics, diversity means something very specific, namely integrating a variety of different races and ethnic groups into the same society or institution. Diversity also refers to integrating women and sexual minorities into institutions that traditionally excluded them, such as the military. Obviously, one can imagine a society without racial and ethnic diversity, but one cannot imagine a society without both men and women. One can, however, imagine a society in which men and women have fairly distinct social realms and roles.

Multiculturalism, multiracialism, feminism, and the LGBTQ agenda constitute the primary sense of diversity today. The people promoting it often have very little use for diversity of opinions and freedom of choice. This politically correct version of diversity is my focus here.

It is no exaggeration to say that praising diversity is the civil religion of our time. Whereas in the past, it was obligatory for everyone—especially the ambitious and powerful—to pay lip service to Christianity, today people compete to offer the most fulsome praise and heartfelt professions of faith to the God of diversity. Beginning with Bill Clinton, US Presidents—Republican and Democrat—have repeated the mantra that "diversity is America's greatest strength." Not just any strength, but our *greatest* strength.

Even as the military, police, and fire departments lower

standards of physical strength to increase diversity, they proclaim that their true strength lies in diversity itself. Indeed, in 2007, General George Casey, then in command of all US troops in Iraq, proclaimed that "I firmly believe that the strength of our Army comes from our diversity."[1] Not weapons, not technology, not training, not the muscles and character of men, not the unity of a common purpose. But diversity. Let us hope this theory is never tested in battle against a serious opponent.

Even as educational institutions lower admissions and graduation standards, gut curricula of demanding classes, create entire disciplines to give degrees and academic jobs to members of marginalized identity groups, and spend vast sums on minority recruitment and diversity propaganda, they claim that education is stronger than ever because of all the diversity, even though by all objective measures, society is spending more on education and people are learning less than ever before.

The same delusional thinking is rampant throughout every other sector of society: business, religion, charities, the arts, etc.

White Nationalists oppose diversity. We want racially and culturally homogeneous homelands for all white peoples. Because our views go against the whole cultural and political mainstream, White Nationalists need to have a good answer to the question, "What's wrong with diversity?" Here are four reasons why diversity would be a bad thing, even if whites were not threatened with extinction.

DIVERSITY MEANS WHITE DISPOSSESSION

The first and foremost reason why diversity is bad is quite simple. Whenever we talk about increasing diversity in a community or a business or a church or a school, that

---

[1] J. D. Leopold, "Gen. Casey Announces Creation of Diversity Task Force," *U.S. Army*, December 3, 2007.

is always a euphemism for having *fewer white people*. Why in the world would white people think that's desirable? There's really no good answer to that.

So when someone says, "You've got a nice little town here—it's affluent, it's clean, it's friendly—but it lacks a certain diversity," the proper answer is: "So, you think there are too many white people here? What's wrong with white people? Why don't you like white people?"

Now some might respond that they don't wish to *decrease* the number of white people. They just want to *add* some spice. But this reply assumes that there's no such thing as scarcity, so that you can add new people to a community without increasing costs and decreasing benefits to the people who are already there. Yet it is legitimate to ask if increasing diversity will take away opportunities from whites while increasing traffic, crime, alienation, conflict, and other social burdens.

Beyond that, even if someone says he does not wish to decrease the *absolute number* of white people, he is still maintaining that there are too many white people *as a percentage of the overall population*. So demand to know why he wants the white population to be diluted.

If diversity just means white dispossession, then obviously it's a bad thing for white people. Obviously white people were bound to start resenting it. Now we are starting to resist it. White Nationalism is simply the inevitable resistance to the anti-white ethnic cleansing that we call diversity. Welcome to the resistance.

Of course increasing diversity is bad for the native peoples of any land, not just whites. When whites came to Africa, Asia, and the Americas, weren't they just increasing the diversity of the place? My first ancestor to arrive in the Americas set foot in Jamestown in 1612. He was fleeing oppression and poverty. He was trying to build a better life for himself and his family. And he was bringing diversity to the New World. But whites never get any credit for that. It's always described as colonialism and genocide when whites do it. Isn't it just as bad when non-whites do it to us?

DIVERSITY WEAKENS ALL INSTITUTIONS

Diversity, we are told, will strengthen literally everything. Presumably this strength means that every institution touched by diversity will *perform its function better*. Neighborhoods will be better places to live. Governments will better promote justice and harmony. Schools will better educate and train students. Hospitals will better heal the sick. Armies and police will produce more security. Firemen and EMTs will save more lives. Churches will save more souls. Businesses will produce more profits. And so forth.

But this makes no sense. Every institution is defined by its goals. Thus to function well, every institution must find people who are good at promoting its goals. Teachers have to teach. Firemen have to fight fires. Soldiers have to fight enemies. Etc. The primary criterion for hiring and promoting people in any institution is ability to contribute to the institution's purpose. *No institution can be improved by introducing competing criteria of success, like diversity.*

Therefore, as soon as diversity becomes the "greatest strength" of any institution, people will naturally lower its proper standards of success to promote diversity. For instance, soldiers and firemen must be physically strong to perform their functions. But when diversity becomes a value—especially the integration of women into professions requiring physical strength—standards are inevitably lowered, thus weakening the institution in the most important way: by making it less capable of performing its function. Thus diversity is not a strength. It is a weakness.

DIVERSITY IS A SOURCE OF CONFLICT

Diversity is a source of conflict within institutions and

within societies as a whole. These conflicts impede them in performing their proper functions, even if one does not adopt the goal of artificially promoting diversity. A school divided by conflict cannot teach as well as a harmonious one. An army divided by conflict cannot fight as well as a unified one. A society riven by conflict is a less pleasant place to live than a peaceful one.

The idea that any society or institution is improved by diversity is an aberration of the late 20th and early 21st centuries. No serious political philosopher or statesman of the past would have entertained the idea for a moment.

The aim of politics is to create social order and harmony. Basically, it's the problem of getting along with one another. Social life has to deliver net benefits to its participants, or people will go their separate ways, and society will collapse. But beyond that, since we're not just selfish individualists, we need to cultivate social responsibility and investment, so that people work to better society and are actually willing to die to ensure that it is preserved and perpetuated. Those are the great problems of politics: creating social harmony and a deep sense of an identification with the body politic, responsibility to the body politic, willingness to lay down one's life for the body politic.

Now, how does racial and ethnic diversity help with those goals? Imagine you're living on a leafy, idyllic suburban street where lots of children play. However, as the population grows and traffic congestion gets worse, you start noticing a lot of people driving through your neighborhood rather fast. They've discovered that your street is a short-cut from one clogged artery to another, so they're racing through your once peaceful neighborhood, endangering little kids.

You decide to do something about it. You want the city to install speed bumps. To do this, you must first go to your neighbors and get them on your side, so you can go as a bloc to petition the city for speed bumps. But to get your neighbors on board, you need to be able to communicate with them. Wouldn't that be nice? But in America today, there are lots of neighborhoods where you cannot communicate with your neighbors anymore. They don't speak the same language.

Beyond that, even if you speak the same language, you still need to have the same values. White nations are now being colonized by people who are not invested in them at all. They are here simply to take. They come from societies that are characterized by public squalor and private splendor. Inside the walls of their houses, everything is lovely, but out in the streets there are dead dogs and potholes, and that's just fine with them. That's their value system. Try motivating people with that value system to get involved with putting speed bumps on your street, even if they have little kids, even if it might protect them. It's very difficult.

To pursue common aims, you need to *already* have things in common. You need a common language for communication. You need to know each other's minds. But then when you know each other's minds, you've got to have the same values, or you're never going to be able to pursue the same goals.

Diversity undermines all of these things. At a certain point, it becomes impossible to pursue or preserve the many social goods that were created when the United States or Sweden or any other European society was predominantly European, i.e., when people spoke the same language, had the same values, knew each other's minds, and felt they could give to the community because it wasn't going to be an act of unreciprocated self-sacrifice. Increased diversity causes decreased social trust, decreased social commitment, and the destruction of the public realm. That's not good for society.

Thus philosophers and statesmen through the ages have considered racial, ethnic, and religious homogeneity to be enormous blessings. For instance, American Founder John Jay—who had to think more deeply about the sources of political order than Bill Clinton or Barack Obama—noted with pleasure in *Federalist Papers* No. 2 that "Providence has been pleased to give this one connected country to one united people—a people descended from the same ancestors, speaking the same language, professing the same religion, attached to the same principles of government, very similar in their manners and customs . . ." Jay did not even regard Negro slaves or American Indians to be part of the American people. The Founders believed that trying to integrate them into the new system on equal footing with whites would have made the new society weaker, not stronger.

Lee Kuan Yew, the founder of modern Singapore, had to create order in a multiracial society, which led him to embrace authoritarianism, not liberal democracy. In an interview with *Der Spiegel*, Yew stated, "In multiracial societies, you don't vote in accordance with your economic interests and social interests, you vote in accordance with race and religion."[2] Thus democracy in a multiracial context was not consistent with political order, particularly a political order that could pursue a common good. Democracy cannot reliably arrive at a governing consensus unless the people who vote are already quite similar to one another. Without a relatively homogeneous population, order has to be imposed from the top down. Thus as diversity increases, democracy fails.

The ancient verity that diversity causes conflict is also supported by contemporary social science. For instance, Harvard sociologist Robert D. Putnam studied 41 communities in the United States, ranging from highly diverse to highly homogeneous. He found that social trust was

---

[2] "Lee Kwan Yew Interview," *Information Processing*, August 14, 2005.

strongly correlated with homogeneity and social distrust with diversity. He found that even people of the same race and ethnic group trust one another less when they live in diverse communities. After eliminating other possible causes for variations in social trust, Putnam concluded that "diversity *per se* has a major effect."[3] Diversity leads to the breakdown of social trust, which leads to the general decay of social order. Thus, according to Putnam, in diverse communities people trust the government and media less, feel politically disempowered, participate less in politics and community projects, volunteer less, give less to charities, have fewer friends, spend more time watching TV, and feel less happy about their lives.

Political scientist Tatu Vanhanen arrived at similar conclusions from a comparative study of diversity and conflict in 148 countries.[4] Vanhanen found that social conflict is not strongly correlated with differences of wealth and poverty, or with differences between democratic and authoritarian governments. But it is strongly correlated with diversity. Whether they are rich or poor, democratic or authoritarian, diverse societies have more conflict than homogeneous societies, which are more harmonious, regardless of levels of wealth or democratization.

Promoting diversity is a bad way to run any society, even ones not threatened by demographic decline.

THE DEEPEST SOURCE OF SOCIAL HARMONY

Why is diversity a source of disharmony? And why is similarity a source of harmony? Is it entirely a matter of culture, namely a common language and system of values? Or is there something more, something deeper? White

---

[3] Robert D. Putnam, "*E Pluribus Unum*: Diversity and Community in the Twenty-First Century," *Scandinavian Political Studies*, 30 (2007), p. 153.

[4] Tatu Vanhanen, *Ethnic Conflicts Explained by Ethnic Nepotism* (Stamford, Conn.: JAI Press, 1999).

Nationalists argue that the ultimate source of political harmony is not culture. It's genetics.

The civic nationalist idea is basically that we can create a unified and harmonious society out of radically different groups of people if we assimilate them to a common language and system of values. Civic nationalists cling to the idea of assimilation, because without it, they will have to break the dreaded taboo of "racism."

Of course we are not even trying to assimilate immigrants today. We have lost the cultural self-confidence to insist that foreigners adopt our norms and way of life. Beyond that, immigrants are very aggressively trying to assimilate us, one taco at a time. Furthermore, until such time as we regain the self-confidence to try to assimilate outsiders, conservative assimilationists should support a complete halt to immigration. And we have to ask: Do conservatives really want to assimilate our most recent immigrants? Can these people actually improve America or any other white country?

Frankly, I am glad that assimilationism was abandoned when we opened our borders to the Third World. I don't want to assimilate non-whites at all, for the more assimilated they become, the more likely they are to intermarry with whites and to gain power and influence in our societies. Thus it is best that their communities remain as separate and alienated as possible, rather than become entangled with the rest of society. It will make it much easier for them to go home someday.

But even if we regained enough cultural self-confidence to demand assimilation, it isn't an easy thing. Most Americans today are a mixture of different European stocks. Some people think, "Well, that was easy." But it wasn't. Even the most superficial acquaintance with American history teaches us there was enormous conflict when very similar groups came from Europe to the United States.

The people of the British Isles are very similar to one

another genetically and culturally. They even speak a common language. But the Irish were not welcome in America, primarily because of a single cultural difference: Catholicism. But that was enough to create enormous conflict and ill will.

These conflicts were exacerbated when even more culturally different groups came to the United States from Southern and Eastern Europe. Because of these conflicts, the United States passed an immigration restriction act in 1924, not to deal with non-white immigration, which was virtually non-existent, but with white immigration from Europe.

I'm glad that America got through these crises and managed to meld different European immigrant groups into a new people: Americans. I am absolutely opposed to any attempts, even under the guise of humor, to reopen old ethnic conflicts in America. We are all Americans now, and most of the time when white people claim a hyphenated American identity, it is simply a case of a person of mixed European ancestry claiming to be Italian or Irish or Polish because of his surname.

Assimilation also had enormous cultural costs. For instance, Americans used to care passionately about the differences between Protestantism and Catholicism. To assimilate large numbers of Catholic immigrants, Americans eventually simply *stopped caring* about religious differences. We *stopped caring* about a lot of historical and cultural differences between Europeans, just so we could stop fighting over them. Cultural assimilation, in short, erases cultural differences. Ceasing to care about them is a creeping form of nihilism that has alienated us from our ancestors, who would regard us as unworthy heirs who have abandoned their cultural legacy.

So it is absurd to say, "It was a breeze assimilating all these European groups, so let's toss Pakistanis and Somalis into the melting pot!" It was hard enough to assimilate fellow Europeans. So why borrow trouble by importing even more radically different people? There is no selfish benefit or moral imperative that requires us to turn our societies into battlegrounds once again. Especially because this time, it is a battle we cannot win, since radically alien peoples could not be assimilated, even if we tried.

It was possible to assimilate fellow Europeans only because they weren't that different to begin with. The United States never managed to assimilate blacks, American Indians, and Asians, most of whom are merely in America, not part of it. White assimilation was possible because, beyond all our cultural differences, we are *genetically* very similar.

Whites are actually the most genetically similar of all the races, because there were points in time in our evolutionary history when there were very few of us, and we all have common descent. So the genetic differences between Eastern and Western Europe and Northern and Southern Europe are quite small, and this genetic similarity was enough to bridge wide cultural gaps and conflicts.

GENETIC SIMILARITY THEORY

J. Philippe Rushton was an evolutionary psychologist who is best known for his book *Race, Evolution, and Behavior.* He is less well-known for his research in what he called Genetic Similarity Theory.[5] When Rushton introduced the idea to me it was in the context of interpersonal relationships. He said, "Opposites don't attract, and I can prove it with science." But he could just as well have said, "Diversity causes conflict, and I can prove it with science."

Genetic Similarity Theory shows that affection, harmony, and altruism among humans—and living things in

---

[5] J. P. Rushton, "Ethnic Nationalism, Evolutionary Psychology, and Genetic Similarity Theory," *Nations and Nationalism* 11 (2005): 489-507.

general—are functions of genetic similarity. The more genetically similar two creatures are, the more likely they will have harmonious relationships.

The ultimate explanation for this is the biological imperative for genes to replicate themselves. One might think that this imperative would lead to ruthlessly selfish and competitive behavior. But it does not, because the genes that seek to propagate themselves are present in multiple individuals. One shares the most genes with immediate family, fewer and fewer genes with more distant relatives, and some genes with everyone in one's broader ethnic and racial group.

Thus each individual will have a tendency toward cooperative, harmonious, and even altruistic behavior toward those who share more of his genes. Individuals are even capable of sacrificing their lives for their families and communities if it secures the greater propagation of their genes among their fellows.

But the flip side of loving one's own is hostility to outsiders. Thus human beings and other animals are willing to fight strangers to protect the genetic interests of their family, tribe, nation, and race. This is the foundation of politics, and politics by other means, namely war.

The science behind Genetic Similarity Theory is very strong. But we don't actually need Rushton's studies to prove this to us, because we are all familiar with a phenomenon that shows that genetic similarity breeds harmony: identical twins. Identical twins have the same exact genes.

I once met a pair of identical twins, and one of them said something quite touching and memorable. It should be the title of a book about twins. He said, "We're not so much two people as *one egg divided*." That was an indication of the level of harmony between them. Just sitting and watching them converse and interact, you could see that they knew exactly what the other was going to say, what the other was thinking; they could finish one another's sentences. And indeed, studies of identical twins, especially twins raised apart, demonstrate how massive and fine-grained genetic determinism really is, as opposed to environmental and cultural factors.[6]

The greatest harmony between two people is the harmony of identical twins. They know one another's minds in ways that even fraternal twins or ordinary siblings just don't. In fact, if you wanted to create the most harmonious society possible, it would be a society of clones. Of course you would need a bit more genetic diversity if you wanted to have sexual reproduction, but surprisingly little. In Iceland, it was discovered that the most harmonious marriages and the most offspring come from people who are as genetically similar as third and fourth cousins.[7]

Genetic Similarity Theory would predict that the happiest societies in the world are also the most genetically homogeneous. This is certainly true in the case of Denmark, which is routinely rated the happiest country in the world[8] and is also one of the most genetically homogeneous.[9] Genetic Similarity Theory also predicts that as a society increases genetic diversity, it will become less harmonious, unified, and happy. Even if such a society somehow managed to "assimilate" this increasing diversity to a common language and system of values, it would *still* be less harmonious and happy than a genetically homogene-

---

[6] Nancy Segal, *Born Together—Reared Apart: The Landmark Minnesota Twin Study* (Cambridge: Harvard University Press, 2012).

[7] Heidi Ledford, "When Kissing Cousins are Good for Kids," *Nature*, February 7, 2008.

[8] Marie Helweg-Larsen, "Why Denmark Is the Happiest Country," *Live Science*, March 30, 2018.

[9] Genetics Society of America, "Genomic Study of High School Students from Across Denmark Reveals Remarkable Genetic Homogeneity," *Science Daily*, October 11, 2016.

ous society. A society can increase its genetic diversity even by assimilating people of the same race, but the most dramatic increase in genetic diversity comes from immigrants of entirely different races. Increased racial diversity makes a society weaker and less harmonious. Diversity is not a strength at all.

White Nationalism is simply the idea of a society where everybody around you is kin. It is a society where you can understand and trust your fellow citizens. Where you can cooperate to pursue the common good. Where you will wish to contribute to grand projects, even though you might not live to see them completed. Where people plant trees so that future generations can enjoy shade. It is a society in which people feel such a strong identity with the body politic that they are willing to sacrifice their lives for it, if they must. But most importantly, it is a society in which you can feel at home. That's what White Nationalism is about: securing homelands for all white peoples.

Without homelands, our people feel rootless, detached, and alienated. They long to be around people with the same culture, history, and destiny. But it is more than that. They also long to be around people who vibrate on the same deep, unconscious frequencies of white racial kinship that bind us all together. That's what White Nationalism wants to create again for our people.

We stand for brotherhood and belonging. Diversity takes those away. That's what's wrong with diversity.

HOMOGENEITY

White Nationalists believe that the best form of society is the sovereign ethnostate that is racially and ethnically homogeneous. But is homogeneity really possible? The simple answer is: yes. We'll deal with racial homogeneity first, then ethnic homogeneity.

We know that racial homogeneity is possible, since only a few decades ago, almost all of Europe was homogeneously white. Indeed, to this day, significant but shrinking parts of Europe and white diaspora societies—entire towns and entire regions—have no non-whites at all. So it is quite conceivable that within a few decades, by moving borders and populations, we can create racially homogeneous homelands for all European peoples.

But one might entertain some exceptions to complete racial homogeneity.

First, in white colonial societies, there might be non-white aboriginal relict populations that are too small and isolated to constitute independent, sovereign ethnostates. So one might wish to create non-sovereign, ethnic reservations with maximum local autonomy so they can lead their lives as they see fit. But it should be pointed out that there are no aboriginal non-white populations in Europe, so no such accommodations need be made there.

Second, white ethnostates will surely maintain trade and diplomatic relationships with at least some non-white societies, which will lead to both non-white visitors—such as tourists and business travelers—and non-white residents, such as diplomats. Since the republics of science, technology, arts, and letters deal with universal values, they are inherently cosmopolitan. Thus a white ethnostate might also wish to host students, scientists, scholars, and artists from non-white countries, for varying periods of time.

In both of these cases, however, a white ethnostate would keep such populations small enough to be manageable and segregated from the rest of the society, so that any citizen who so desires could completely avoid dealing with racial aliens. This would mean that such an ethnostate could guarantee *de facto* racial homogeneity to every citizen who desires it. Furthermore, every non-white living in such a society would accept and live by white norms of behavior. This is the exact opposite of today's multiculturalism, in which whites are expected to abandon our norms and practices whenever aliens demand it.

This leads us to a threefold distinction:

- ❖ *Strict homogeneity*—meaning the complete lack of racial or ethnic outsiders
- ❖ *De facto homogeneity*—meaning that even if outsiders are present, they are segregated so that the vast majority of people—all of them that want to—live in a *de facto* homogeneous society
- ❖ *Normative homogeneity*—meaning that even if outsiders are present, they accept the norms of the society and act accordingly

Any ethnostate could establish complete racial homogeneity, if it wanted to pay the price. But if a society does not want to go that far, it can still guarantee *de facto* homogeneous living spaces for all citizens who want them, and then can uphold and enforce normative homogeneity, i.e., the hegemony of white values, for whites and non-whites alike.

Complete ethnic homogeneity, like complete racial homogeneity, is possible in principle, if one wishes to pay the price. But achieving ethnic homogeneity is much trickier than racial homogeneity. In Europe, one can simply repatriate all non-whites to their ancestral homelands. But that would leave a Europe in which political borders seldom map out neatly along ethnic borders. One could rectify this situation by breaking up multinational states and moving peoples and borders around. But all of these solutions are much more costly than removing non-white interlopers, simply because the primary costs must be borne by our fellow whites.

We believe that breaking up multinational states on ethnic lines—for instance in Yugoslavia, Czechoslovakia, Belgium, Spain, France, or the UK—is the best way to resolve ethnic conflicts and preserve ethnic diversity. There are two ways of attaining this end: the easy way and the hard way, the velvet divorce of the Czechs and the Slovaks, or the wars and ethnic cleansing of the Balkans.

But as the Scottish and Catalan referendums revealed, many people's nationalistic impulses are invested in preserving multinational states, even from the secession of peoples they disdain as backwards, inferior, Left-wing, and decadent. We can only hope that these sentiments ebb as the tide of ethnonationalist thinking continues to rise.

Imagine, then, a Europe in which the most serious ethnic tensions have been resolved by secessions, partitions, and—where necessary—population exchanges. Even in such a Europe, there will still be ethnic minorities: Swedes in Finland, Hungarians in Romania, Poles in Lithuania, etc. There will also be Europeans who wish to work and study in other European countries, Europeans who marry people from other nations, and Europeans who might wish to retire in warmer climes. Also, because misfortune can befall every society, international law should require every sovereign state to make provisions for refugees from natural disasters, wars, and oppression.

Similar conditions will pertain in European colonial societies, with the added difference that they might also have non-white aboriginal relict populations.

What should our attitude be toward people from other white nations?

Ethnonationalists wish to preserve distinct European cultures and subracial types, which is the whole point of having distinct homelands in the first place. We do not want to see the emergence of a homogeneous European man or a white monoculture. Therefore, policies toward other white nations must bear this goal in mind.

The aim of preserving distinct nations dictates the following.

No white society should allow large populations of guest workers from other white societies, or create conditions that lead large numbers of its own people to search for work abroad.

Immigration between white societies should be limited. Practically all cases would be due to marriage. The naturalization process should firmly promote normative homogeneity, i.e., assimilation of the dominant language and culture by immigrants and especially by their children. It is possible for Europeans to join other European nations, and even if they might not be able to fully assimilate, their children certainly can.

Ethnic minority groups should be allowed to retain their own languages and cultures. There should be no forced assimilation, as there was under civic nationalist regimes, since this simply creates conflict. But by the same token, minorities create a great deal of resentment by refusing to learn the dominant language and demanding that the state cater to them by instituting bilingualism. Again, the principle should be normative cultural homogeneity, meaning that outsiders need to abide by the local language and customs. If they find this oppressive, they have homelands to which they can move.

Expatriates from other white nations should be allowed, in limited numbers, as long as they respect the dominant culture and the natives need not interact with them.

No nation can simply turn away refugees, because some day its people may need to seek refuge in other lands. But white nations are under no obligation to take in non-white refugees, which can go to other non-white countries. White refugees, however, should be welcomed and helped until such time as they can return to their homelands. In the case of refugees who have no homelands they can return to, like white Rhodesians and South Africans, they should be offered the chance to immigrate. Depending on their destination, they could be given the option of assimilating to the dominant culture or becoming a distinct ethnic minority.

As for tourists, business travelers, diplomats, students, scholars, artists, and scientists: the same policies should pertain to those from white countries as to those from non-white ones. Their numbers should be limited, they should respect the dominant culture, and the natives should be completely free to avoid them if they so choose.

To maintain racial distinctness, ethnostates should have laws against miscegenation. These are obviously more important in colonial societies with non-white relict populations, but they should exist in all white societies to prevent people from trying to bring home non-white spouses.

The main objection to compromising on absolute racial and ethnic homogeneity is that it seems like a slippery slope toward civic nationalism. But this is a mistake. Civic nationalists hold that people of radically different races and cultures can become part of the same society simply by professing a civic creed and taking an oath. That is a very thin conception of identity.

Ethnonationalists have a much thicker sense of identity based on both genetic kinship and enculturation. The primary cultural marker that sets ethnic groups apart is different native languages. But it is *hard* to become fluent in another language—and even then, it will never replace one's mother tongue.

Civic nationalists believe that it is very easy to become a member of another society. Ethnonationalists believe that it is difficult if not impossible. It is impossible for non-whites to become members of white societies. It is difficult for whites to become members of other white societies. It is easier, of course, if an immigrant and his new homeland share the same native tongue and basic culture—for instance, the countries of the Anglosphere. But the greater the linguistic and cultural differences, the greater the difficulty of assimilation, to the point that full assimilation is often possible only for the children of immigrants, who should be raised to speak the dominant language as their mother tongue.

Not only do ethnonationalists think that cultural assimilation is difficult, they only insist on it for immigrants. For visitors and temporary residents, white and non-white alike, as well as for white minority groups living within their borders, *ethnonationalists do not want or encourage assimilation.* Instead, they wish different groups to maintain their cultural identities and simply *accommodate* the dominant culture by respecting its norms and by speaking the dominant language in public dealings. Of course travelers and temporary residents will have some latitude in these matters, but permanent residents should be held to higher standards. Not everyone within a given country at a given moment might be a citizen (which is homogeneity in the strict sense), but all of them should respect its laws and culture, which is the meaning of normative homogeneity.

One might object: Isn't normative homogeneity just

cultural chauvinism or supremacism? It is not necessarily chauvinism, because chauvinism is a conviction of superiority. We do not insist that foreigners speak our language and follow our customs because we think they are superior. We insist upon it *simply because they are our own*, and we set the rules in our homeland just as we set the rules in our individual homes. And as for supremacism: Can anyone explain to me why our language, culture, and norms should *not* be supreme in our own homelands?

One might also object: Isn't the idea of *de facto* homogeneity just another version of the gated community, where people flee from diversity in order to enjoy life among their own kind? An ethnostate can indeed be likened to a gated community, but there's nothing wrong with that. First of all, we need to have a proper understanding of what a gated community is. Even in gated communities, outsiders come and go: visitors, deliverymen, tradesmen, etc. But they have to follow the local rules, and they can't enter private homes without permission. So residents don't have to deal with them if they don't want to. A normatively homogeneous ethnostate functions in the exact same way: outsiders come and go, but only by permission; they have to follow the local rules; and residents do not have to deal with them if they don't want to. So within an ethnostate, even though there might be outsiders, the citizens come first, and there is a commitment to allowing them to live without any contact with outsiders whatsoever, if that is their choice. This is what it means to have *de facto* racial and ethnic homogeneity within an ethnically defined society.

To many, the idea of complete racial and ethnic homogeneity will seem utopian. As we shall see in the next chapter, this is untrue. To others, it will seem extremist, fearful, and ungenerous. This is indeed true. But the fear that motivates us is the prospect of racial and cultural extinction—a fear which, as we have seen above, is completely reasonable. A race facing genocide cannot afford to indulge in sentimentality, moderation, and half-measures.

At minimum, the survival of our race requires an end to non-white economic competition, political power, and the promotion of intermarriage in white homelands, and the best way to accomplish that is complete separation. Perfecting the ethnic homogeneity of white nations is a far less pressing matter. The price of not pursuing white homelands is extinction, and compared to that prospect, what we lose by going to extremes is negligible. What critics call going to extremes is simply what White Nationalists call erring on the side of caution.

However, once whites feel that we have a future again, we will be able to take the risk of accepting less than fully homogeneous societies, although they should always be on our own terms, meaning that we should always insist on normative and *de facto* homogeneity, which will still create levels of intelligibility, community, and belonging far beyond what most white people can enjoy today.

WHITOPIA

> "... the US Constitution poses no serious threat to
> our form of government."
>
> — Joseph Sobran

Utopianism is one of the most common objections
leveled against White Nationalism, even from people
who largely agree with us.

The word *utopia* literally means *nowhere* and refers to
an ideal form of government that is not actually found
anywhere in the world and may be impossible to realize. For the vast majority of persuadable whites, utopianism flatly disqualifies any political ideology, and the
tiny minority that finds grandiose and impossible-
sounding utopian visions appealing are overwhelmingly Leftists, the vast majority of them implacable enemies
of white self-determination. Thus to own the label *utopian* is self-defeating in the extreme.

Fortunately, there is no need to paint ourselves into
the utopian corner, because the ethnostate is no mere ab-
straction. *De facto* ethnostates exist on the planet today:
Poland and Japan, for instance, are overwhelmingly racially and ethnically homogeneous, and although neither
makes ethnicity the explicit legal foundation of citizenship, they consistently reject proposals to open their borders to mass immigration. Tiny Estonia, although afflict-
ed with a large foreign population descended from Russian colonists, is a *de jure* ethnostate, for its constitution
explicitly claims that the primary aim of the Estonian
state is the preservation of the Estonian people for all
time.

Within the United States, we know exactly what a
homogeneously white society would look and feel like,

because there are countless places in which there are no non-whites at all, or such tiny numbers that they do not alter the norms and functioning of white society. These communities include many of the suburbs and resorts favored by our anti-white elites. These "whitopias" are quite real, and they are routinely ranked among America's best places to live. The goal of White Nationalism is Aspen, or Chappaqua, or Martha's Vineyard for everyone.

Moreover, within the lifetimes of many present-day Americans, the kinds of laws and policies favored by White Nationalists actually existed, from immigration laws designed to preserve the white majority, anti-miscegenation laws to maintain racial purity, eugenics laws to improve future generations, and even mass deportations of Mexican invaders from border states. These are not utopian pipe dreams. They have already happened. Indeed, some of these laws even seem too radical for present-day White Nationalists.

Thus the first step to creating a White Nationalist America is to dust off these laws and policies and implement them once again. America could become a normatively white society again tomorrow. That is simply a matter of will. And once that decision is in place, we can adopt and improve upon tried and true policies to move from multiculturalism toward the white ethnostate. This process might take fifty years. But we could take our time to get it right, because whites would begin to reap enormous psychological benefits today, simply by knowing that our people have a future again.

The ethnostate is no utopia. We know that ethnostates are possible, because they are actual. The real utopia is the multicultural, multiracial paradise where diversity is a source of strength, not alienation, inefficiency, hatred, and violence. Pursuing the multicultural utopia is making vast parts of the white world into dystopias. Compared to multiculturalism, White Nationalism is sober, plodding political realism.

So if the ethnostate is a real possibility, aren't White Nationalists obligated to spell out exactly what kind of society it will be? Will it be capitalist or socialist? Will it be democratic or authoritarian? Will the legislature have one house or two? What will the flag look like?

Many White Nationalists are dismissive of such questions, and for good reasons.

First, such questions are premature. It may be generations before we have white ethnostates in North America, and the task of designing institutions will fall to future generations. It seems hubristic to try to make decisions for them.

Second, it is naive to think that there is one right answer to these questions. A glance at history reveals an astonishing variety of different political regimes in white societies. Different white peoples find different forms of government attractive. A Scandinavian ethnostate might be much more socialistic than an American one, but they could be equally committed to the survival and flourishing of their citizens.

Third, it is imperative for the White Nationalist movement to unify as many whites as possible around the idea of the ethnostate. However, demanding agreement on the details of the ethnostate is the quickest way to get White Nationalists fighting one another. Thus the more specific our proposals for the ethnostate, the less likely we are to get any kind of ethnostate at all.

Fourth, such questions put too much faith in institutions and laws, and not enough faith in our people. Whites have a way of creating decent societies, no matter what political and economic systems we adopt. Conversely, as the history of post-colonial Africa proves so abundantly, even the wisest constitutions cannot produce good government if the people are not capable of it. Thus the most important thing is for white nations to regain control of their demographics and their destinies. Once this happens, we can simply trust the white genius for self-government to come up with a whole range of workable political models.

As convincing as these arguments are, however, White Nationalists still have to offer at least some specifics. White Nationalism will never happen unless we can rally as many whites a possible to our cause. But if we offer no concrete proposals, we are in effect asking our people to give us a blank check, and most of them will quite understandably balk at that.

Focusing, for example, on the United States, White Nationalists need to adopt the following policies to turn America into an ethnostate.

First, we need to close our borders to non-white immigrants.

Second, we must repatriate all post-1965 immigrants and their descendants to their ancestral homelands.

Third, we must deal with pre-1965 non-white populations by offering them, for instance, autonomous reservations, independent ethnostates, or resettlement in their ancestral homelands.

Fourth, we must create barriers to race-mixing. The best anti-miscegenation policy, of course, is simply creating a white homeland. But since it is impossible to prevent all inter-racial contact—due to tourism and trade, for instance—we also need strong social norms and even laws to discourage miscegenation.

Fifth, an ethnostate must institute pro-family policies. We must restore biologically-based and tradition-hallowed sex roles: men as protectors and providers, women as mothers and community builders. We must also make it affordable for men of all social classes and income levels to own homes and support housewives and children.

Sixth, we will have to adopt protectionism and pro-labor policies to promote the return of high-wage manufacturing jobs to America.

Seventh, we will have to reform our educational system, culture, and media to purge them of anti-white propaganda and to communicate the knowledge, skills, and virtues necessary both to flourish as individuals and perpetuate our civilization.

Beyond these specific policies, we can also predict certain features of future White Nationalist societies because they are already part of the White Nationalist movement today.

For instance, the White Nationalist movement is religiously pluralistic, so any White Nationalist society we create will be religiously pluralistic and tolerant.

The White Nationalist movement allows civic participation by women, so that will also be part of the society we create in the future.

Finally, the White Nationalist movement rejects the bourgeois idea that the highest values are material comfort, security, and a long life, because these values make people slaves of the anti-white system that rules us. Thus when we create a White Nationalist society, it will never allow bourgeois values to trump racial idealism.

All White Nationalist policies require government action. They are not going to happen simply by leaving people alone. The trends we are trying to reverse were created by bad government policies, and they can only be reversed by better government policies. White Nationalism by its very nature is statist rather than libertarian, collectivist rather than individualist, illiberal rather than liberal. We believe that there is a common good—

the survival and flourishing of our people—which can only be promoted by government policy, and we believe that whenever private interests conflict with the common good, the common good must win out.

This much is obvious. What people want to know is just how far this collectivism and anti-liberalism will go.

The political mainstream, particularly in the United States, is divided between the Left, which has no trouble using government to promote anti-white policies, and the Right, which tends toward a naive distrust of government as such and a naive faith that social order can spontaneously emerge from the bottom up.

Our enemies on the Left will not attack our statism, they will attack our aims. Our enemies on the Right might even share some of our aims, but they will attack our statism, and they will do so by likening White Nationalism to the worst forms of totalitarianism: Stalin, Hitler, Orwell's *Nineteen Eighty-Four*, etc.

The best response to this sort of straw man argument is to point out that all of the policies we advocate actually existed, to one extent or another, in the United States within the last century, when the country was far freer and happier than under the present, politically-correct multicultural system.

Indeed, although America's current egalitarian civil religion has deep roots, the idea that the American nation was founded to promote equality for all mankind is a false, Left-wing revisionist construct—as I argue in my essays, "Is White Nationalism Un-American?" and "What Is American Nationalism?"[1] Indeed, Americans had the good sense to resist racial egalitarianism throughout most of their history.

The Declaration of Independence may state that "All

---

[1] Both reprinted in *Toward a New Nationalism.*

men are created equal" — which is simply a denial of hereditary monarchy, not a statement of blanket human moral or factual equality — but Thomas Jefferson, the author of those words, believed that although blacks may indeed have the same inalienable rights as whites, the two races could not exist free and equal in the same society. Thus he supported repatriation of freed slaves to Africa.

The Declaration, moreover, is not a legal document. The fundamental law of the land is the Constitution, which says nothing about universal human equality and does not treat non-whites as part of the American people.

According to the Constitution, the purpose of the American government is not to promote human rights for all mankind, but to provide good government "for ourselves and our Posterity." When the first congress passed the Naturalization Act of 1790, it specified that only free white persons could become part of the American people.

The United States did not allow blacks to become citizens until 1868. Foreign born blacks could become citizens only after 1870. American Indians who did not live on reservations could become citizens in 1868. Citizenship was granted to all American Indians only by the Indian Citizenship Act of 1924. Chinese immigration began in the 1840s but was banned from 1882 to 1943, and Chinese born in America were not considered citizens until 1898. Only in 1940 was naturalization opened to people of Chinese, Philippine, and East Indian descent, as well as Indians and mestizos from other parts of the Americas. But each extension of citizenship to non-whites was fiercely resisted. Probably none of them would have passed if the people had been allowed to vote on them directly. Moreover, until 1965, American immigration laws were designed to maintain a white supermajority with an ethnic balance based on the 1890 census.

A free, white homeland is every American's birthright. And for all of America's ideological errors and political compromises, most Americans enjoyed a *de facto* white homeland until the 1960s. But this birthright was stolen by capitalists who wanted cheap labor, liberal universalists who wanted to save the world, and Jewish ethnic activists who wanted to dilute the white majority. American White Nationalists are not utopians. We simply wish to restore every white American's birthright.

White Nationalism is no mere abstract possibility. Everything we advocate has already been tried. We know White Nationalism is possible, because it has already been actual. Thus the burden of proof is on the advocates of multiculturalism—which has never improved any society anywhere—to prove that their vision will lead to anything but hell on earth for white people.

The desire for White Nationalists to produce written constitutions also ascribes too much importance to written documents. The US Constitution is a masterpiece of political thought, but is it actually the foundation of the American political system? No, not really. The best way to appreciate this is to compare America and England, which are quite similar in their cultures, laws, and political institutions. Yet England has no written constitution at all. By contrast, the Constitution of Liberia that was in effect from 1847 to 1980 was based closely on the US Constitution, but Liberia hardly resembles the United States in its culture and government.

The foundation of the English system of government is not a piece of paper, but a people and its traditions. The American system is similar to the English because it is an offshoot of the same people and traditions. The US Constitution is less the foundation of the American system than an attempt to articulate and summarize important features of the English political tradition and its nearly two centuries of divergent evolution in the American colonies. This tradition, and the people who created and sustained it, are the true foundations of the American system of government.

This truth has been obscured by the idea that the Constitution is the foundation of our political system, although even the strictest constitutionalists admit that the Constitution cannot be interpreted without reference to the intention of the framers and the culture of the time. Moreover, the example of Liberia shows that there is no civilizing magic in the Constitution alone. The US Constitution could never be successfully grafted onto a radically different people, with radically different traditions of government.

The relative powerlessness of constitutions—both written and unwritten—is underscored by the fact that virtually every European government today has adopted policies of race-replacement immigration, a course of action so perverse that the wisest of legislators could not have foreseen and forbidden it. Indeed, they would have been mocked as insane if they had even suggested the possibility. Moreover, white genocide has become policy without fundamentally altering the written or unwritten constitutions of European societies. Time-hallowed parchments and institutions did not stop the rise of anti-white regimes. But, by the same token, they cannot stop the return of pro-white regimes either.

For pro-white regimes to return, however, we have to understand the true foundation of political power. Political constitutions are no better than the people who interpret and apply them. Political institutions are no better than the people who staff them. Thus politics depends on something that lies *outside* of politics, namely *metapolitics*, which is the topic of the next chapter.

POLITICS, METAPOLITICS, & HEGEMONY

"Public sentiment is everything. With it, nothing can fail; against it, nothing can succeed. Whoever molds public sentiment goes deeper than he who enacts statutes, or pronounces judicial decisions."

—Abraham Lincoln

Epictetus begins his *Handbook* of Stoicism with an essential distinction, "Some things are in our power, and some are not." Wisdom is knowing the difference. This is true in individual life, and it is true in politics. The goal of the White Nationalist movement is the power to reshape society. But that is not in our power today. To gain the power we want, we must use the power we already have.

Let's call the things we can't control "social conditions." The things we can control are our own actions. Social conditions in the Anglosphere and Western Europe are much less favorable to White Nationalist politics than in Central and Eastern Europe. But these conditions can change dramatically and unpredictably. Thus we must do everything in our power to build up our movement, so that we are ready if changing circumstances give us the opportunity to make headway.

Our enemies command more wealth and coercive power than any regime in history, although they rule primarily through propaganda and other forms of soft power. Their greatest weaknesses are false ideas and decadent values that are leading to terrible consequences. These catastrophes and the subsequent attempts to cover them up, explain them away, and avoid blame are shredding their credibility. Our enemies are also enormously cynical, corrupt, degenerate, and frankly laughable.

Our strengths and weaknesses are almost the mirror image of those of our enemies. We lack their wealth and coercive power. Our greatest advantage is that we stand for a true worldview and healthy values that offer real solutions to the problems of diversity and white demographic decline; we also enjoy the credibility that comes from speaking the truth. We are also far more idealistic than our opponents (although our movement currently has its share of cynicism, corruption, degeneracy, and buffoonery). In short, we can never outspend our enemies. We can never defeat them in armed combat. But we can beat them in the battle of ideas.

Our greatest opportunity is the system's reliance on propaganda, because the Internet and advances in software and computing now make it possible for White Nationalists to produce and distribute high-quality counter-propaganda at ever-diminishing prices. We are changing people's minds, and the system is powerless to change them back.

In the United States, all of the successes of the White Nationalist movement have been on the metapolitical rather than the political plane. "Metapolitics" refers to the non-political preconditions of political change. To secure these conditions, we must engage in: (1) *education* and (2) *community organizing*. Education refers to making the intellectual case for a new political order, as well as creating media to propagate that message. Community organizing refers to the creation of an actual, real-world community that lives according to our principles.

Basic metapolitical ideas include questions of *identity* (who are we, and who isn't us?), *morality* (what are our duties to ourselves, our nations, our race, and other nations and races?), and *practicality* (how can we actually create white homelands?). This entire book is an essay in metapolitics.

Institutions and communities that exercise influence over the political realm are also metapolitical. These include educational and religious institutions, the news and entertainment media, organized ethnic and economic lobbies, and secret, unaccountable cabals now loosely referred to as "deep states."

To understand how metapolitics shapes politics, we must make a distinction between "hard power" and "soft power." Hard power is political power, which is ultimately backed by force. Soft power is metapolitical power, which influences politics in two ways. Metapolitical ideas shape people's beliefs about what is politically possible and desirable. Metapolitical organizations shape political policies while remaining outside the political realm.

If political power ultimately comes from the barrel of a gun, metapolitics determines who aims the gun, at whom it is aimed, and why. If political power is "hard" power, because it ultimately reduces to force, metapolitical hegemony is "soft" power that ultimately reduces to persuasion. Persuasion, of course, is not just rational argumentation but also emotional manipulation and economic carrots and sticks, including simple bribery and blackmail.

One of the crucial distinctions between hard and soft power centers on the idea of *accountability*. Hard political power is, at least in theory, accountable to the people. Political accountability ultimately means that the people who make political decisions are *known* to the public and can be *punished* for betraying the public trust.

The exercise of soft power has no such transparency or accountability. Soft power allows the destinies of nations to be shaped by individuals whose identities and agendas are obscure and who are essentially unaccountable for the consequences of their actions. Indeed, they are often foreigners, with no ties and loyalties to the nations they manipulate.

Another term for metapolitical soft power is "hegemony." The Greek word *hegemonia* means leadership, domination, or rule *exercised at a distance*. Hegemony is *remote control*. Specifically, for the ancient Greeks, hegemony referred to imperial or federal leadership, in which the *hegemon* rules over other states with regard to foreign and military affairs but leaves domestic matters in their hands. For the man in the street, therefore, hegemony appears as a distant, indirect, mediated, "soft" form of power.

Hegemony can also take an intellectual and cultural form, ruling over the political realm by shaping the values and ideas that set the boundaries and goals of political debate and activity. For instance, the hegemony of anti-white, pro-multicultural ideas in American politics today means that it really does not matter which party holds power, since their power will be used against white interests. But the converse is also possible: If White Nationalist ideas attain cultural hegemony, it will not matter which party holds political power, since all of them will treat white interests as sacrosanct.

The concepts of metapolitics and hegemony are the keys to understanding the differences between the Old Left and the New Left—and the Old Right and the New Right. By the Old Left, I mean Bolshevism. By the Old Right, I mean interwar National Socialism, Fascism, and similar regimes. The Old Right emerged in reaction to the Old Left. The Old Left sought to impose Communism through one-party politics and the totalitarian state, using terrorism and genocide as tools of policy. Just as one takes a knife to a knife fight and a gun to a gunfight, the Old Right used the Old Left's chosen weapons to resist it. The Old Right fought violence with violence, hard political power with hard political power.

The New Left—the best example being the Frankfurt School—replaced politics with metapolitics, the hard totalitarianism of the Old Left with the soft totalitarianism of Leftist cultural hegemony. The New Left realized that

Leftist values could be imposed without a violent revolution and a totalitarian, one-party state, simply by taking control of education and culture. One can have total social hegemony while maintaining the illusion of freedom and pluralism by ensuring that all competing cultural currents and political parties adopt the same Leftist values, differing only on inessential matters.

The New Left was wildly successful. Today we live in a Left-wing, soft totalitarian society, which Jonathan Bowden characterized as a "Left-wing oligarchy," a system of vast economic and political inequities in which everyone piously mouths Left-wing slogans.

Just as the Old Right took guns to a gunfight, the New Right must take ideas to a battle of ideas. We must deconstruct the hegemony of anti-white ideas and replace them with a counter-hegemony of pro-white ideas. We must create our own metapolitical organizations—new media, new educational institutions, and new forms of community—that can combat and replace those in anti-white hands. We must fight bad ideas with better ideas, institutional subversion with institutional renewal.

A metapolitical approach also plays to our strengths. The moral, scientific, and historical case for White Nationalism has never been stronger, even though we lack money, organization, and political power. The enemy, by contrast, has never been richer, better organized, or more politically powerful. But they have never been weaker on moral, scientific, and historical grounds.

Two political models that have wide appeal in the broader White Nationalist community are useless in this metapolitical struggle: libertarianism and Old Right-style White Nationalist organizations, which are now referred to as White Nationalism 1.0. Both approaches tend to view politics as solely a matter of hard power. They also tend to overlook or underestimate the role of soft power.

Libertarians oppose the exercise of hard power by the

state, which is in principle accountable to the common good, but they have absolutely no problem with unaccountable soft power as long as it is exercised by private actors. Libertarians oppose government censorship but have no problem with corporate censorship promoted by private organizations like the Anti-Defamation League and the Southern Poverty Law Center, which draw up politically correct terms of service and employment to be adopted by institutions and compile lists of dissidents to be silenced by social media, fundraising platforms, web hosting providers, and financial services companies. The only objection a libertarian could have to total Jewish media domination is if the checks bounce. Otherwise, it's all "voluntary." Libertarians can, however, be counted on to oppose any government regulations to stop corporate censorship and deplatforming. Thus libertarianism not only blinds people to the workings of soft power, it opposes on principle any use of government force to curb it.

As for the Old Right's contemporary imitators, they spend their time imagining race war scenarios in which armed revolutionary parties defeat the United States government, as outlined in the novels of William Pierce and Harold Covington—and the more impatient and antisocial types occasionally go on shooting rampages. When Communists and anarchists LARP[1] as Bolsheviks, the Old Right shows up with helmets and shields to LARP as Nazis.

Although the intellectual and moral case for White Nationalism has never been stronger, and the intellectual and moral case for multiculturalism has never been weaker, White Nationalists cannot defeat the armies, police, or even the mall cops of modern societies in armed struggle. It is the height of strategic folly to abandon our greatest strengths and refuse to attack the enemy where he is

---

[1] Live-Action Role-Play.

weakest, and instead attack the enemy on the plane of hard power, where he is strongest and we are weakest.

This is not to say that there is no room for street activism today, but it has to be understood as a metapolitical activity, a form of propaganda, not as a battle to control the streets. The best examples of this approach to activism are the Identitarian Movement in Europe and the American Identity Movement in the United States. Actual politics comes later, once we have laid the metapolitical groundwork.

To conceive of White Nationalism as politics without metapolitics—as simply a struggle for political power, regardless of whether the people sympathize with us or not—basically puts us in the position of an invading army or an unpopular revolutionary party, which seeks to conquer the state and impose its will on the people. This is the trap of the Old Right model.

The opposite extreme is metapolitics without politics, but this approach actually has a chance of working. If White Nationalists attain complete hegemony in the metapolitical realm, that means that white interests will be sacrosanct, and anti-white ideas will be anathema. In such a situation, White Nationalists need not organize as a political party to capture the state, because we will have captured the minds of the public, and all the existing political parties will be *de facto* White Nationalist parties, because they will serve white interests.

In such a society, we would still be arguing about abortion and taxes, but it would be an argument between white people alone. There would be no possibility of allying with non-whites to gain short-term political advantage over our own flesh and blood, and the degradation and destruction of our race would simply be outside the realm of political possibility. Frankly, this would be "whitopia" enough for most of us.

In practice, of course, the political and metapolitical

paths to power work in tandem. Even an armed takeover by a revolutionary party would presuppose metapolitics in order to create an ideological consensus within the party itself. And even if White Nationalism became the common sense of the whole society, we would seek to make that victory permanent by organizing to take control of governments and other institutions and oust anti-whites from all positions of power and influence.

How can white identity politics make its way from the margins to the mainstream? White Nationalists often debate "vanguardist" vs. "mainstreaming" approaches to politics. Vanguardists believe we have to lead the public to our views. Mainstreamers want to make our views closer to the public's.

There are two things we can do to make our ideas more mainstream. We can change their substance, or we can change their style, i.e., the way we communicate them. Obviously, it is self-defeating to change the substance of our beliefs to fit the mainstream. Indeed, the whole point of our movement is to change the mainstream to fit our beliefs. The vanguardists are simply correct about this.

But although our core principles should be fixed and non-negotiable, we should be willing to be quite suave, supple, and pragmatic in the means by which we communicate them if we hope to convince the largest possible number of our people. In this, we have much to learn from the mainstreamers.

In my view, there are four political absolutes that White Nationalists cannot compromise on:

1. Europeans constitute a distinct race, the white race. Thus to be French or German or Swedish or Greek or Italian or Irish is also to be *white*. Whiteness is a *necessary condition* of being part of any European nation. Therefore, no non-racial form of civic, linguistic, cultural, or reli-

gious nationalism is sufficient to defend European peoples.

2. The white race is threatened with simple biological extinction, compared to which all other political issues are trivial distractions. White extinction, moreover, is the predictable result of political policies. So we are facing not just extinction but genocide. Only by recognizing the absolute and ultimately *political* nature of the threat can we define a real solution and create the necessary moral seriousness and urgency to implement it.

3. The only tenable solution to the threat of white extinction is White Nationalism: the creation of homogeneously white homelands for all white peoples, which will require moving borders and people.

4. Jews are a distinct people and belong in their own homeland. This last point is really a self-evident implication of the principle of ethnonationalism, but it needs to be spelled out because Jews wish to exist both in an ethnostate and as a diaspora. The organized Jewish community is also one of the principal architects of the policies we wish to change, and one of the main impediments to correcting them.

How can White Nationalists change the whole of white society? We need to persuade as many of our people as possible of the points above. Then we need to mobilize them to change the political order.

To persuade as many whites as possible, we have to reach out to as many whites as possible. We need to convince whites from all walks of life: every age group, every social class, every religion, every ethnic group, every interest group, every subculture—everyone. We need to take stock of the full diversity of the white community. Then we need to craft a version of White Nationalism that appeals to every white constituency. White society is like a great coral reef, and White Nationalists need to colonize every niche with a customized version of our message.

Obviously, the best people to sell White Nationalism to every white subgroup are members of that group. Thus our movement must encompass the full diversity of our people, interact with and persuade the full diversity of our people, and then draw the whole of white society toward us.

It sounds impossible. But we know it is possible, because it has been actual. We don't have to go too far back in the history of any European country before we find that the very ideas we advocate today were hegemonic.

Moreover, the historical moment has never been more receptive to white identity politics. More people are looking to us for answers than ever before. Thus we must develop new platforms, spokesmen, and messages to try to reach and convert them. And we must do it now, before the moment is lost.

So what can we do to accomplish this? How can we encompass such an immense and multifarious undertaking in a single movement?

To answer this, we need to make a distinction between hierarchical organizations and non-hierarchical social networks. The existing White Nationalist movement has many organizations, and would-be organizations, with internal hierarchies: leaders and followers, employers and employees. But these organizations are not the movement. They are mere nodes in a vast non-hierarchical network of organizations and individuals, which is the true movement.

This movement was not created and guided by some mastermind. Instead, it coalesced out of many independent voices that created platforms for themselves or colonized existing ones. Moreover, the growth of our movement has far more to do with the failures of multiculturalism than our own efforts at propaganda and organization. Events are arguing in our favor better than we are.

Again, we must always remember that some things are in our power, and some are not. None of us has the power to organize the movement from the top down. But all of us have the power to help the movement flourish from the bottom up, if we can discover and follow rules of behavior that will allow our movement to grow in power and influence, until it can turn the world around. This is the topic of the next chapter.

A WINNING ETHOS

The White Nationalist movement is more like a subculture than a political party. It is a network of individuals, web platforms, and organizations. It exists more online than in the real world. We hope this subculture will give birth to political change. But before we can change the world, we need to be the kind of movement that can actually do that. So it is worth asking what sort of ethos would make us more likely to win. Here are a few simple rules that will give us an edge. If we follow them consistently, they will make our movement increasingly formidable.

POPULISM & ELITISM

White Nationalism is *populist* in the sense that we believe that a regime can be legitimate only if it represents the common good of a people, meaning the interests of the whole body politic, not just a single part. Populism does not mean engaging in folksy, lowbrow pandering to below-average people. That's just an elitist parody. Populism represents the whole body politic.

White Nationalism is also *elitist*, because it turns out that the best way to represent the interests of the whole body politic is through an elitist movement. We need to attract the *best* of our people to fight for *all* of them.

Every society is ruled by elites. The only question is whether they rule in the interests of all, or in their own interests. Currently, white nations are ruled by the wealthiest, most powerful, and most diabolically evil elite in human history. When Plato and Aristotle compiled their catalogs of bad forms of government, neither of them imagined a regime so evil that it was dedicated to the replacement of its own population with foreigners. Our rulers are also astonishingly degenerate, delusional, and corrupt. But we are still no match for them in a purely political struggle.

To beat our current elite, White Nationalists will have to become an even more formidable elite. Therefore, *all* of our people will be better off if we can attract the *best* of our people to our movement. We want to recruit people who are above average in intelligence, education, idealism, altruism, income, taste, and social capital. We are not snobs. We will recruit the best people, no matter what their class origins. But we will not win if we imitate skinhead street gangs and other groups that recruit from the left side of the white bell curve.

How do we organize a movement that constantly attracts better and better people—a movement that continually reaches higher levels—and then surpasses itself?

The first step is to set high standards and maintain them. White Nationalists are often quite paradoxical. In theory, we are highly elitist. But in practice, we have almost infinite tolerance for profoundly defective people. The motivation is understandable: Racially aware people are rare, so we treasure anyone who comes our way.

But we need to have more faith in our message: Virtually all white people have the capacity for racial awareness and pride. We are just ahead of the curve. But people of quality will not be receptive to our message, much less contribute to our movement, if we coddle defective and repulsive people. *Every inferior person keeps one hundred better people from joining our cause.* And again, we will be more likely to build a movement that can represent the interests of all our people if we are highly selective about our membership.

Once we have set high thresholds for entry, and floors below which people cannot sink, we still have to think about ceilings. We don't want them. We don't want any upper limits on the evolution of our movement. This is why we need to be quite wary of would-be leaders, because someone who relishes the role of leader a bit too much will want to surround himself with inferiors—flatterers and flunkies—and try to run off genuinely superior people who might challenge his status. The best leadership material is someone who never seeks followers but instead seeks people he would like to follow.

Fortunately, the White Nationalist movement is not a unified, hierarchical movement that needs a single leader. Instead, it is a network of individuals and organizations. Every organization needs hierarchy and leadership. But the movement as a whole doesn't. Not yet, anyway. Given the danger that a single leader would cap off the upward evolution of the movement, I would rather the average quality of movement people to be a lot higher before we risk that.

In the meantime, instead of waiting around for leaders, we should work to create a movement that can attract a genuinely great leader. Finding such a person is largely a matter of luck. It is not something we can control. But we can control whether or not we are a movement *worthy* of a leader. So until a leader appears, figure out how you can contribute as much as you can. Because if you are hanging back, watching and waiting for a leader before you start contributing to the cause, that might be self-defeating. Without your efforts, the movement may never attract the kind of leader you are waiting for.

BASIC COURTESIES

One of the highest priorities of the White Nationalist movement is to destroy the taboo against white identity politics. The only way to overthrow a taboo is to *openly* defy it. A taboo retains its power if people reject it in private but not in public. Thus, if the movement is to triumph, we need *explicit* White Nationalists.

However, there are serious social consequences for being explicit White Nationalists. People can lose their jobs, families, and social capital. Thus it is inevitable that the first waves of explicit White Nationalists will tend to be people who are psychologically eccentric and have little to lose.

The movement will never win, however, unless we can gain the support of people who are more average in their psychological profiles and above average in their education, income, social capital, etc. Unfortunately, these people have the most to lose from associating openly with White Nationalism.

Therefore, if our movement is to grow powerful enough to win, we also need to make a place for *secret agents*, who can contribute surreptitiously to the movement without destroying their normal lives. The movement would be weaker, not stronger, if everyone in a vulnerable position doxed himself and allowed the system to destroy him. To bring such people into the movement, we need to respect their desire for privacy by following two simple rules:

1. Each individual gets to determine his own level of explicitness and involvement.
2. Everybody else must respect those decisions.

The first principle recognizes that each person is ultimately responsible for his own security and privacy. Online and in real life, one will inevitably encounter both enemy infiltrators and sincere kooks and cranks. Both groups are quite dangerous. So each individual needs to determine his own balance of caution and risk.

The second principle amounts to a plea to be charitable in interpreting people's motives for being discreet. People of good character have good reasons for being discreet. People of quality are not going to join a movement swarming with paranoids who accuse them of the blackest motives—cowardice, treason—for protecting their identities. Sensible people will fear doxing and back slowly out of the room.

However, even though we must always respect people's decisions to remain anonymous, we must always try to get people to expand their comfort zones: to do more for the cause, and to do so more explicitly. When we win, it will be safe for everyone to be an explicit White Nationalist. Before we win, it will be risky. But we will never win without people who are willing to take risks. We will *encourage* people to take more risks. But we will never attract people of quality unless they are certain that *we will not presume to take risks for them.*

As a reciprocal courtesy, White Nationalist secret agents need to observe two rules as well:

1. There's a reason why the first wave of explicit White Nationalists tends to be people who are eccentric and have very little to lose. Don't rub it in.
2. Don't harp on security concerns excessively, especially in public, lest you make yourself and others paranoid, which undermines our efforts to encourage greater openness and commitment.

PROMOTING COOPERATION & AVOIDING SECTARIANISM

Right now, White Nationalism is a movement of the Right. But we will win when white identity politics becomes the common sense of the whole culture and the whole political spectrum, Left, Right, and center. That day will come sooner if we can cooperate with wider and wider circles of racially-aware whites. Some of the benefits of cooperation include:

- ❖ learning from the experiences—and mistakes —of others
- ❖ not wasting scarce resources duplicating the ef-

forts and competing with the events and products of other nationalists. We need carteliza-
tion, not destructive competition.
- ❖ adjudicating disputes in an equitable—and
quiet—manner, or avoiding them altogether
- ❖ collaborating with one another to accomplish
tasks too great to accomplish on one's own

To make such cooperation possible, we simply have to
learn to work with people who share our views of white
identity politics but may not share our views on a whole
range of other issues. And as our movement grows more
successful in penetrating and changing the whole culture,
white identity politics might be the *only* thing that unites
us.

Of course we will continue to have passionate opinions
and disagreements on other topics. But we need to be
willing to set these aside to work with others for the
greater good of our race. That one simple trick is the key
to ensuring the broadest possible cooperation and coordi-
nation among white advocates, creating a movement that
is larger, more powerful, and more likely to be able to save
our race.

The principal enemy of such cooperation is what I call
sectarianism. There are people who insist on combining
White Nationalism with a list of Right-wing add-ons—
Christianity, paganism, radical Traditionalism, holocaust
revisionism, etc. Furthermore, they insist that these peripheral issues are essential to white preservationism, thus
they turn them into polarizing litmus tests and shibbo-
leths. This approach is guaranteed to create a smaller,
weaker, dumber, poorer, and less effective—but more
"pure"—movement, when we need to go in precisely the
opposite direction.

Such behavior is often dismissed as "purity spiraling."
But purity is not a problem. The problem is failing to dis-

tinguish between what is essential and what is peripheral to white identity politics. We should keep our core principles pure. The mistake is to demand purity on marginal matters as well.

There is a difference between a political ideology and a political movement. A political ideology is defined by philosophical first principles. A political movement is defined by its goals and assessment of political realities. It is possible for people to join the same political movement for a wide variety of ideological reasons. Insisting that we all have the same reasons is the source of sectarianism.

If our movement is to grow, we need to discourage such sectarian tendencies. Currently they are of the Right, because that's where our movement began. But Left-wing sectarianism will inevitably emerge as our movement grows to encompass the whole political spectrum.

Doing away with sectarianism will also do away with endless silly debates about "purges" and "entryism." A political party needs to worry about entryism and can conduct purges. But White Nationalism is mostly a virtual movement with no clear boundaries between "inside" and "outside." So it can neither guard itself against entryists nor purge dissenters. All of that is empty talk when anyone can become a "member" of our movement simply by setting up a forum account, and when anyone can become a "leader" simply by starting a website, podcast, or YouTube channel.

DISAGREEMENT & COLLEGIALITY

The pro-white movement should be as pluralistic as the society we are trying to change. We will be united by our common goal of racial salvation. But we will have all sorts of differences on less essential issues, like style and tactics, as well as the inevitable personality clashes.

So how do we handle these disagreements?

One suggestion in our circles is that we should never

fight among ourselves. We should never "punch right" or disavow one another but instead present a united front to the world. This seems reasonable. When you are under attack, you should strive to unify your camp and sow discord among your enemies.

But there are important caveats.

First, there is a difference between physical fighting and the battle of ideas. If our people are being assaulted, doxed, or persecuted by the state, we should always rally to their aid, regardless of differences of personality or principle. (Of course we should only come to the aid of *innocent* victims. If we come to the aid of reckless people with a record of getting into trouble, that creates a moral hazard, and we cannot allow such people to monopolize scarce resources.)

Second, in the battle of ideas, there is no sense in demanding that we present a united front, particularly on issues where there are real disagreements of principle. It is not "divisive" to sincerely disagree with someone. Again, our aim is the hegemony of pro-white ideas. We wish to change the whole cultural and political spectrum. Which requires that we *engage* the whole cultural and political spectrum. But this means that we cannot agree with each other on every issue, nor can we hide our disagreements. Indeed, declaring our disagreements is how we differentiate our approaches before the public.

Our movement needs to cultivate many different voices addressing many different audiences and employing many different strategies. So obviously they can't all say the same thing. We have to disagree with each other openly. We have to set boundaries openly. We have to criticize one another openly. Being open and frank about our differences is, therefore, essential to the growth of our cause.

Moreover, our movement today is primarily intellectual and cultural. Spirited debate is the life-blood of such movements. It is what makes us more interesting and attractive than the cultural mainstream, where the life of the mind is stifled by political correctness.

But there are good and bad ways of stating disagreements. The good way is to adopt a civil and charitable tone, to give the most generous possible reading of an opposed position, and then offer sound reasons (facts and valid arguments) for the superiority of one's own view. The bad way is to adopt a paranoid and aggressive tone, to give jaundiced readings of opposed positions, and to play fast and loose with facts and logic. There should be no taboos on criticizing other people and positions in the movement. The only taboos should be against bad ideas, bad arguments, bad manners, and bad faith.

Principled intellectual disagreement, defending yourself from attacks, and calling out people for harming the movement are all legitimate grounds for public debates. Pointless and merely personal vendettas are not.

But doesn't refusing to shy away from disagreements in our ranks contradict the principle of avoiding sectarianism? Not really. Again, there is a difference between a political movement and an ideological sect. A political movement is defined by its goals and analysis of political realities. An ideological sect is defined by its first principles. It is possible for people to support the same political movement for many different reasons. Spirited but civil debate about those reasons actually makes our movement more attractive to the people we are trying to convert.

It only becomes a problem if people cannot set aside those disagreements when it is time to work on common tasks. The virtue of *collegiality* is what allows people with differing opinions to work together for the common good. Collegiality is particularly important in our movement, since it is the kind of cooperation that exists between independent actors, as opposed to people in hierarchical organizations, who can simply be ordered around. Collegiality is what allows professors, prelates, and politicians to stop debating and start working together when necessary.

The lack of the concept of collegiality is one reason why people in our movement wish to enforce taboos against debate and disagreement, since they cannot grasp that intellectual debate can be combined with practical collaboration.

One reason our movement is so fractious and uncollegial is that we lack common projects and a sense of forward momentum. The 2016 Trump campaign was the high point of movement collegiality. Once we recover that sense of common purpose, momentum, and optimism, people will be more willing to work together.

IDEALISM, DEDICATION, & SELF-SACRIFICE

A perennial question debated by American Rightists is: "Why does politics continually drift to the Left?"[1] This indicates that Leftists have a systematic advantage over the Right. I believe that advantage is essentially *moral*.

But the Left is evil, and the Right is good, so how can the Left have a moral advantage over the Right? Because Leftists are capable of mobilizing moral virtues for evil ends. Leftists are on average more idealistic, dedicated, and self-sacrificing than Rightists. They are willing to work harder and sacrifice more to bring about their ideals. And other things being equal, the team that can muster these to a greater degree will win.

The main stumbling block of the Right is bourgeois morality. The bourgeois ethos holds that the highest good is a long, comfortable, secure life. By contrast, the aristocratic ethos holds honor as the highest value, to which the aristocrat is willing to sacrifice both his life and his wealth.

---

[1] See Greg Johnson, "Metapolitics and Occult Warfare," in *New Right vs. Old Right* (San Francisco: Counter-Currents, 2014).

(Bourgeois man, by contrast, is all too willing to sacrifice his honor to pursue wealth and extend his life.) The bourgeois ethos is also opposed to the willingness of idealists to die for principles, whether religious, political, or philosophical. The Left, even though its value system is entirely materialistic and unheroic, still manages to mobilize idealism and heroism because it contemptuously negates bourgeois man.

As a movement, we need to cultivate idealists who take principles seriously and warriors who are willing to fight and, if necessary, die for our people. Only these people have the moral strength to begin pulling the political spectrum back towards the Right—or, better, in a pro-white direction.

In his *Dedication and Leadership*, former Communist Douglas Hyde offers some valuable suggestions for recruiting and cultivating political idealists.[2]

First, young people tend to be idealistic, so special efforts should be focused on recruiting them.

Second, if you want to *get* a lot from people, *demand* a lot from them. The US Marine Corps has no shortage of recruits because their recruitment propaganda emphasizes sacrifice and discipline, not the perks of membership.

Third, aim high. If one is going to ask people to commit their all, one has to give good reasons. Grandiose aims are only a problem if there is nothing concrete one can do in the here and now to realize them. But if one can forge that link, then even the humblest drudgery suddenly takes on a deeper and higher meaning.

I once asked a group of White Nationalists why they had gathered. There were many answers: meeting new people, networking, seeing old friends, etc. These reasons were good enough to get them there. But then I offered a

---

[2] Douglas Hyde, *Dedication and Leadership* (South Bend, Ind.: University of Notre Dame Press, 1966).

better reason: to save the world. White Nationalists are not just struggling to save the white race, since the welfare of the whole world depends upon our triumph. If we perish, so will the whales, so will the condors, so will the tigers, so will the rainforests. So the next time you attend a White Nationalist gathering, remind yourself that you are saving the world. It will make the commute a little easier, the parking less of a hassle.

Demanding heroic dedication to a higher cause does not drain people but energizes them. It does not hollow out their personalities but deepens them. Those who live for themselves alone have less meaningful lives than those who dedicate themselves to a higher cause.

Fourth, be the best possible version of yourself. There is no contradiction between being a good White Nationalist and being good in every other area of one's life. If you are going to be a good White Nationalist, you also have to be a good student, worker, employer, artist, spouse, parent, and neighbor.

One is a more credible and effective advocate for White Nationalism if one is well-regarded in other areas of one's life. Personal relationships with exemplary individuals are generally more important than ideology in recruiting new people to a political cause.

Also, if one finds that political commitments are interfering with excellence in other areas of life, then one needs to scale back and regain balance. This prevents activists from burning out and keeps them in the fight.

Only idealism can jumpstart a movement. Only idealism can sustain it through hard times. But a movement that depends *entirely* on idealism will burn through people and fail. Thus we also have to build *personal rewards* into activism. We need to offer friendship and community; we need to pay people for their work, not just rely on volunteerism; we need to create economically self-sustaining institutions, not just charities; we need to counter the armies of professional blacks, mestizos, and Jews with some full-time professional white advocates.

THE INTENSITY GAP

In "The Second Coming," W. B. Yeats brilliantly describes a decadent culture on the brink of collapse. Two lines are especially relevant to our cause:

The best lack all conviction, while the worst
Are full of passionate intensity.

For Yeats, civilization is always imperiled by the forces of chaos. The best are the defenders of civilization, the stoppers in the mouth of hell. The worst are the rabble that would tear civilization down if given the chance. What happens when the best no longer feel a passionate attachment to civilization? What happens when such men have to fight against a rabble animated by passionate intensity? Obviously, other things being equal, the underworld will be unleashed, the rabble will triumph, and civilization will fall.

The same disparity exists in our movement today. During my nearly two decades on the White Nationalist scene, I have seen disaster after disaster caused by energetic cranks and kooks. They could have been stopped. But the better men in the movement lacked the conviction and emotional intensity necessary to oppose them.

Our movement will never amount to anything unless the best among us learn to wed good character and judgment to passionate emotional intensity.

Today it is the modern multicultural system that is decadent and teetering on the brink of destruction. Today it is the *worst*—our ruling elites—who increasingly lack all conviction. This is an enormous opportunity. For if the best of us can put our movement on the right course, and muster sufficient emotional intensity, then—other things being equal—we can win.

THE RELEVANCE OF
THE OLD RIGHT

What is the relevance of what I call the Old Right—
German National Socialism, Italian Fascism, and related
interwar national-populist movements—to White Nationalism today? The question would not even arise, of course,
if there were no connection at all. Many White Nationalist
ideas are either direct descendants of Old Right ideologies, or they are their cousins, meaning that they share
common ancestors, that they are branches of the same
ideological tree.

This is what I take from the Old Right:

1. *Nationalism over globalization*: The Old Right
   put the preservation and flourishing of historically existing peoples ahead of the imperatives
   of universal ideologies like liberalism and
   Communism and the homogenizing tendencies
   of globalizing institutions like the marketplace.
2. *The common good over individual liberty*: The
   Old Right put the health of the body politic
   ahead of individual freedom and self-expression.
   One can still value liberty, private life, individ-
   uality, and private enterprise, but only to the
   extent that they promote a healthy society.
3. *Biology is central to politics*. Liberal individualism simply does not care about the demographic or dysgenic trends it establishes, because caring about such things is "collectivism." The Old
   Right saw that the health of the body politic
   has everything to do with long-term demographic trends, and it took the responsibility of
   promoting positive rather than negative ones.

Thus the Old Right promoted strong family bonds, healthy population growth, and encouraged the healthiest and most intelligent to have large families.

4. *Whiteness is a necessary condition of European identity.* There is more to being a Frenchman or a German than merely being white, but no non-white can be a Frenchman or a German or a member of any other European people. Thus we cannot preserve European nations without preserving their racial basis.

5. *Jews are a distinct people who therefore belong in their own homeland, rather than scattered among European peoples.* And if that were not reason enough to separate ourselves, Jews have a long history of promoting values and policies that are objectively harmful to whites.

Of course, since all of these ideas are based ultimately on reality, they are not unique to the Old Right. The first three principles, for instance, were simply political common sense before the Enlightenment. One could arrive at all five of these principles based on one's own experience and reasoning, or through other intellectual and political traditions. Thus, there is no *necessary* connection between modern day White Nationalism and the Old Right. And that is the proper answer to those who wish to dismiss White Nationalism by linking it to the Nazis or Fascists: *not necessarily.*

For instance, in my own intellectual biography, I arrived at the first three principles through the study of classical political philosophy. I arrived at race realism and awareness of the Jewish question through observation, conversations with friends, and reading books like Richard J. Herrnstein and Charles Murray's *The Bell Curve* and Kevin MacDonald's *The Culture of Critique.* And it was only on the basis of that background that I could see truth and value in the Old Right.

Of course this does not imply that I learned nothing from the Old Right. First, the Old Right *made sense* within my worldview. Then it *added to* my worldview. But it never *became* my worldview. And that same worldview also gave me some critical distance from it as well.

White Nationalism differs from the Old Right in three principal ways.

First, we are *universal nationalists*, meaning that we believe that ethnonationalism is good for all peoples. Thus we oppose imperialism, whereas Old Right regimes practiced imperialism against their fellow Europeans as well as non-whites. Defending imperialism is basically telling your neighbors that you are not above a little murder and theft when it suits you. But that is no way to build solidarity among white nations or a peaceful planet in general, to the extent that these are possible.

Second, given that White Nationalists today are concerned with the well-being of our race, both as a whole and in all its constituent ethnic parts, it makes no sense to identify White Nationalism with any particular Old Right regime, since those regimes pursued their particular national interests at the expense of other European peoples. For instance, identifying White Nationalism with German National Socialism is a self-defeating tactic when dealing with Poles or Ukrainians, regardless of the fact that a minuscule minority of these nations are broadminded enough to share such attitudes, or at least tolerate them.

Third, the Old Right was born in the struggle against Bolshevism, and it adopted the Bolsheviks' organizational model and tactics to beat them, e.g., the paramilitary party and the totalitarian state, including terrorism and mass murder as tools of policy. Imitating such policies today, however, is ineffective (to say nothing of moral considerations). The postwar hegemony of the Left was not established by Bolshevik means but through institutional and cultural subversion. Thus the New Right must combat them through institutional and cultural renewal. This is the basis for the metapolitical strategy of the New Right. New Rightists do not object to taking a gun to a gunfight, but we do object to taking a gun to what is now essentially a battle of ideas.

In sum, the Old Right is highly relevant to White Nationalism in terms of its analytical framework and political goals, but we reject imperialism in favor of universal nationalism and the Bolshevik organizational model and methods for metapolitics.

So how should White Nationalists today approach the Old Right? The same way we should approach any tradition or body of thought: with an open but critical mind. First, get enough education and experience to form your own worldview, understand who you are, and exercise adult judgment. Then, standing on that foundation, examine the Old Right, incorporate what is true and useful, reject what is not, and move on. This approach requires self-awareness, authenticity, and groundedness in one's own identity and worldview.

The least productive engagement with the Old Right is when people who lack a worldview of their own go shopping for a complete and ready-made system of ideas that they can adopt as a package deal. Common examples in our circles include Catholicism, Orthodoxy, Traditionalism, and National Socialism. Old Right ideas are adopted essentially as religious dogmas, in which one defers to the thoughts and judgments of others rather than developing one's own.

The danger is that such people will latch on to and repeat ideas and strategies that are no longer justified—if they ever were—and they will lack the experience and critical thinking skills necessary to get beyond them. They also lack the groundedness in present-day reality necessary to apply such ideas productively. The usual result is the strident, brittle, and quarrelsome people who populate Internet forums and comment threads. However, trying ideas on for size is part of intellectual growth and exploration, and exposure to experience and counter-arguments generally tends to mature such people.

Another unproductive engagement with the Old Right is not just adopting a ready-made system of ideas but imaginatively identifying oneself with the Third Reich or another bygone fascist regime. This goes well beyond learning the lessons of history to apply them to the present and instead becomes escapism, a way of fleeing from the present rather than transforming it, a way of re-fighting the battles of the past, which cannot be changed, and avoiding the battles of the present, in which our race's future is at stake. To accuse such people of LARPing is usually an undeserved compliment, because such role-playing seldom leads to "live action" of any sort.

There is also something deeply inauthentic about identifying with a past regime, especially if it is a foreign one. White Nationalism is a form of identity politics. To be real identity politics, however, it has to be based on a *real* identity. We are not just creatures of our own time and place, since we reject the false and meaningless identities that the current system offers us: deracinated individuals, citizens of the universe, children of nowhere, defining ourselves by the products we consume and discard. Instead, our identity is defined by our whole biological and cultural lineage, which leads to the present day and cannot be re-routed to some other time and place.

We reject the modern "identity" because it is false, because it does not fit us, because it makes us miserable and base. But modern individualism can only be fake if we *already* have a real identity, although we might be largely unconscious of who we really are. Therefore, the answer to the modern malaise is to discover who we are and live accordingly, to be authentic rather than fake. It is no answer to simply replace the predominant fake identity with something equally fake but merely more eccentric or marginal. Adopting off-the-rack systems of ideas or living in the past are symptoms of rootlessness rather than solutions for it.

Fortunately, White Nationalists of every nation do not have to look too far back in the history of their own homelands to find prominent sages and statesmen who believed what we believe today. Many of the laws we propose were already on the books in most white countries. An authentic ethnonationalist movement needs to graft itself onto the living traditions of its own homeland, not exotic imports or toxic and highly stigmatized ideologies.

Contra those who would pretend that the Old Right never existed, it has much to teach us. But it is part of the past. It is dead, and it needs to stay that way. Those who would revive it are guilty of a number of serious errors: *anachronism*, because we are now in a battle of ideas; advocating patently *immoral* policies, such as imperialism; *rootlessness and inauthenticity*, for identifying with foreign ideologies and nations rather than seeking a basis for nationalist policies in their own political traditions[1]; and finally *self-marginalizing, self-defeating behavior* at the very moment when the broad public has never been more receptive to our ideas. We need to get serious, before we lose the historical moment and our race slips beyond the point of no return. Many Old Right revivalists sense this burning urgency, but if we don't have time to do the right thing, doing the wrong thing won't save us anyway.

---

[1] In the case of the Germans, however, they have to be highly selective about appeals to their own Rightist traditions.

AS INEVITABLE AS
WE MAKE IT

White Nationalism is the inevitable reaction of whites who are being ethnically cleansed from our homelands. Of course most people are not so vulgar as to explicitly call for the ethnic cleansing of whites. Instead, they use euphemisms like "diversity" and "multiculturalism." Whenever a business, a church, a school, or a neighborhood becomes more "diverse" or "multicultural," that simply means fewer whites and more non-whites.

Replacing non-whites with whites is never lauded as diversity or multiculturalism. When it happens in a non-white neighborhood, it is decried as "gentrification." When it happens in a non-white country, it is condemned as "imperialism" and "colonialism," or even "ethnic cleansing" and "genocide." Non-whites get to keep their spaces, but whites don't. What is theirs, they keep. What is ours, is negotiable.

Since diversity means nothing more than the replacement of whites with non-whites, which is ethnic cleansing, and all the leading institutions of our society are actively promoting diversity, obviously a reaction was inevitable.

To appreciate that fact, we don't need to go into the arguments for or against diversity. We don't need to talk about biology, history, sociology, or economics. We don't need to know which side is right. All that can come later. Right now, all we need to recognize is that whites, like any other healthy animal, will fight back when we feel that we are being attacked.

When whites become aware that we are being attacked as a group, other political issues—including the most contentious issues that divide us—seem less important. Conversely, what we have in common—our racial and ethnic identity, the target on our back, which we can't pull off because it is part of us—becomes more important.

In a homogeneous society, politics is about differing conceptions of the common good, because in a homogeneous society, citizens have a great deal in common. We often take this for granted. Indeed, we seldom even notice it until diversity and multiculturalism are thrust upon us.

In a multicultural society, the only things that people have in common are a territory and a political and economic system, in which organized groups that do share a common identity fight against one another for power and resources.

White Nationalism is identity politics for white people, and it will inevitably arise when formerly white societies become multiracial societies. It will only cease when multiracialism is replaced with racially and ethnically homogeneous white societies again.

White Nationalism, at minimum, is white identity politics within the context of a multiracial society. Whites will inevitably organize to preserve our wealth, power, and communities from non-white depredations. Such White Nationalist politics need not even be explicitly racial. In fact, when White Nationalism first emerges, it is seldom willing to directly confront the taboo against racial identity, so it embraces civic rather than racial nationalism and pursues white interests under the guise of universal principles like rights and legality.

Nevertheless, even the most sheepish and bashful, even the most self-contradictory and self-defeating White Nationalist sentiments were powerful enough to carry the Brexit referendum and propel Donald Trump to the US presidency. Indeed, such implicit White Nationalism is the animating principle of the growing National Populist movements across the white world.

As National Populists rack up victories, we will inevitably move from implicit to explicit racial advocacy, and we will switch from defense to offense. We will not just halt white dispossession, we will reverse it. We will demand nice white neighborhoods, schools, businesses, communities, and countries—and getting those requires replacing non-whites with whites.

At this point, White Nationalism will come to a fork in the road. The left fork will preserve multicultural societies, but put whites firmly in charge and restore white super-majorities. This is the white supremacist option, to which civic nationalists are logically committed, because to them the right fork is morally and politically frightening.

The rightward route embraces the deepest meaning and impetus of White Nationalism. It rejects diversity entirely in favor of the idea of the ethnostate. It is willing to move peoples and borders to create racially and ethnically homogeneous homelands for all European peoples who aspire to self-determination. This is the ultimate aim of White Nationalism as I conceive it.

Europe is the motherland of our race. No other race has any legitimate claim on it. Thus there is absolutely no reason why the nations of Europe should not remove all non-whites. In the case of the United States and other European settler societies, fairness demands some accommodation for the remnants of indigenous peoples and the descendants of black slaves, preferably by giving them autonomous homelands.

In the case of the US, I am willing to entertain civic nationalist approximations to the ethnostate as temporary, expedient compromises with political reality. For instance, I believe that White Nationalists should seriously promote a new immigration/emigration policy that aims to return to the ethnic *status quo* of 1965, which was in many ways the peak of American civilization. The goal would simply be to erase the catastrophic error of opening our borders to the Third World. This transformation could take place gradually, with 2065 as the target date for completion. This sort of proposal could even meet with the approval of many non-whites, because it gives a place to their kind in America's future. As long as whites had complete freedom to disassociate with other races, the result would be a *de facto* White Nationalist society for the vast majority of whites.

But there is no guarantee that such a racially segregated society would not eventually grow complacent, then delusional and profligate, repeating all the mistakes that are destroying us today. Thus White Nationalists will have to keep moving the goalposts toward the complete realization of the ethnostate. There's no reason for us to ever stop extolling the idea of a completely homogeneous society, because even the most timid civic nationalists know, in their heart of hearts, that America would be a better place with no blacks or Mexicans or Muslims whatsoever.

Whether White Nationalism ultimately leads to segregated white supremacist societies or homogeneous ethnostates depends on historical contingencies that cannot be predicted or controlled. It is also possible that White Nationalism will fail entirely in some countries.

But we can say that White Nationalism is inevitable, because it *already* exists, even though its ultimate victory is uncertain. We do not appeal to pseudo-scientific notions of inevitable historical progress, like Marxists. And although many of us take inspiration from Traditional and Spenglerian cyclical views of history, we also believe that it is our duty to *fight* for a Golden Age rather than to give in to decline or to count on historical forces to do our work for us.

In the beginning, White Nationalism is as inevitable as an abused dog biting its tormentor. Beyond that, victory is only as inevitable as we make it.

There is good reason for optimism, however, simply

because racial and ethnic diversity within the same society are sources of disunity, conflict, and the erasure of distinct identities. Anti-white ethnic cleansing can only be maintained by lies and moral blackmail—and, when these fail, by intimidation and outright violence. One can flout reality for a long time, as long as you can make other people pay the price. But eventually, multicultural regimes lose their strength through division and chaos and their legitimacy through lies and broken promises.

By contrast, since White Nationalism is in harmony with reality, our strength will only grow, because we understand that it arises from racial and ethnic unity, and our credibility will only grow, because it is based on speaking the truth. Indeed, because the best evidence of our superiority will be provided by the system itself, White Nationalism will in essence feed off the system's decline.

The current establishment is already working feverishly, at nearly 100% capacity, to suppress white identity politics and white racial consciousness, which are just beginning to stir. But this means that our ethnocentrism has far more room to grow than their capacity to contain it. Thus even a small spike in white racial consciousness might overwhelm the system's ability to suppress it, at which point all bets are off.

Eventually the trajectories of their decline and our rise will cross, and when our rising consciousness exceeds their declining ability to control us, then we win.

THE VERY IDEA OF
WHITE PRIVILEGE

I want to thank Frodi and the rest of the Scandza team for making this event possible, as well as all of you for coming out to hear me. I am honored today to be speaking alongside these distinguished doctors of the human sciences. My Ph.D., however, is in philosophy. Philosophers don't do scientific research. Instead, we stand back and try to talk about the big picture, including the meaning of scientific discoveries for politics and morals. My topic today is "The Very Idea of White Privilege."

A *privilege* is an advantage that you enjoy and others don't. Privilege is inherently unequal. Special privileges are the opposite of equal rights. *White privilege* means advantages enjoyed by whites just in virtue of their race—rights not enjoyed by non-whites. White privilege is a form of *hereditary* privilege. Whites do nothing to earn or merit white privilege over and above simply being born. White privilege thus refers to a whole range of unequal and unearned—and thus unjust—advantages enjoyed by whites and denied to non-whites in the societies that whites created. White privilege is just another word for white "racism."

The concept of white privilege has exploded in American public discourse in the last five years, coinciding with the so-called "great awokening," the wave of Left-wing hysteria and gaslighting set off by the Trayvon Martin and Michael Brown hoaxes, namely the claims that two blacks who were killed while committing crimes were actually the real victims, innocent victims of white racism.

The concept of white privilege has provoked a great deal of eye-rolling and healthy anger from whites. This manifestation of white toughness has, absurdly, been termed "white fragility," which is a clear sign that the Left is not just out of touch with reality but simply thinks that it can be conjured up or banished with word magic.

Whites reject the idea of white privilege for various reasons.

- ❖ Some think that racism is a terrible thing, but they don't think that they or their societies are guilty of it.
- ❖ The vast majority of white people work very hard and never had anything given to them, so they resent the idea that they benefit from un-earned privileges.
- ❖ Others think there is nothing wrong with racial inequality and believe that white privilege is just another politically correct moral swindle in which non-whites seek unearned advantages by accusing good-hearted whites of spurious of-fenses for which they can buy forgiveness.

But as much as I applaud this pushback against white privilege, the concept is not entirely meaningless. For in-stance, within the lifetimes of some people present today, whites enjoyed legal privileges denied to non-whites in Apartheid South Africa and the American South.

But there is not a white society in the world today in which whites enjoy such legal privileges over non-whites. Even the idea of nationality through descent is being chipped away as a form of privilege. Indeed, in South Afri-ca and the United States, non-whites now enjoy privileges over whites, both legally and through massive private dis-crimination.

Yet, even with decades of official and unofficial non-white privilege behind us, certain non-white groups are more likely than whites to be uneducated, poor, and in

trouble with the law—to name just three important factors in overall social well-being.

The official explanation for these lingering inequalities
is "racism," that is to say: white malevolence, as well as
"systemic" forms of inequality. According to this theory,
since all people want to thrive in white societies and have
equal inherent potential to do so, the fact that some
groups conspicuously do not thrive needs to be explained.

Since white people are the architects of these societies,
we are obviously the ones to blame. Thus white people
must be hectored and browbeaten and reeducated. We
must be punished by affirmative action and reparations.
And we must endure having our societies torn apart and
rebuilt over and over again, until racial equality is attained. Because nothing stands in the way of racial equality except white institutions and ways of life, white ignorance and ill-will, white guilt and white privilege—or so
they say.

But it is increasingly difficult to believe this viewpoint
because white legal privileges have been overturned.
White privilege has not, moreover, been replaced by a
classical liberal meritocracy, in which all people are subject to the same rules and judged on individual merit, but
by a system of non-white privilege. But even with the system rigged in their favor, some non-white groups conspicuously lag behind whites in a vast number of indexes
of social well-being.[1]

Even though anti-racist activists and non-whites find it
increasingly difficult to point to any specific cause of persistent inequality, they *just know* that it is *somehow* white
people's fault. This is why the Left has resorted to increasingly "occult"—i.e. hidden and mysterious—explanations

---

[1] An excellent summation of these differences is Richard
Lynn's *The Global Bell Curve: Race, IQ, and Inequality Worldwide*
(Augusta, Ga.: Washington Summit Publishers, 2008).

for persistent racial inequality.

Since fewer and fewer whites are *consciously* racist, the problem must be *unconscious* racism *somehow* keeping certain groups down. Unconscious racism is a real phenomenon, but how far does it explain persistent inequality?[2]

Since fewer and fewer whites hold negative racial stereotypes about other groups, and non-whites are still displaying stereotypical behavior, non-whites must be sabotaging themselves because of the "threat"—the mere specter—of negative stereotypes existing in their own minds. And this is still white people's fault, *somehow*.

Since explicit, legal racism has been dismantled and even reversed, the legacy of past racism must still exert a subtle influence that is powerful enough to cancel out the effects of much more recent systems of non-white privilege, *somehow*.

The classic statement on white privilege is Peggy McIntosh's 1989 essay, "White Privilege: Unpacking the Invisible Knapsack," where she writes:

> I have come to see white privilege as an invisible package of unearned assets that I can count on cashing in each day, but about which I was "meant" to remain oblivious. White privilege is like an invisible weightless knapsack of special provisions, maps, passports, codebooks, visas, clothes, tools, and blank checks.[3]

McIntosh offers fifty examples of white privilege. McIn-

---

[2] On unconscious racism, see Kevin MacDonald's "Psychology and White Ethnocentrism," *The Occidental Quarterly*, vol. 6, no. 4 (2006).

[3] Peggy McIntosh, "White Privilege: Unpacking the Invisible Knapsack," *Peace & Freedom Magazine* (July/August 1989), pp. 10–12.

tosh's backpack is more of a grab bag, ranging from discrimination in housing and law enforcement to the color
of band-aids. McIntosh's examples make it very clear that
when she speaks of non-white Americans she is thinking
specifically of black Americans.

Most of McIntosh's white privileges fall into two broad
categories: (1) aspects of having a homeland, and (2) not
being black. Aspects of having a homeland include:

1. I can if I wish arrange to be in the company of
people of my race most of the time.

2. I can avoid spending time with people whom I
was trained to mistrust and who have learned to
mistrust my kind or me.

6. I can turn on the television or open to the front
page of the paper and see people of my race widely
represented.

7. When I am told about our national heritage or
about "civilization," I am shown that people of my
color made it what it is.

8. I can be sure that my children will be given cur-
ricular materials that testify to the existence of their
race.

12. I can go into a music shop and count on finding
the music of my race represented, into a supermar-
ket and find the staple foods which fit with my cultural traditions, into a hairdresser's shop and find
someone who can cut my hair.

14. I can arrange to protect my children most of the
time from people who might not like them.

15. I do not have to educate my children to be aware of systemic racism for their own daily physical protection.

16. I can be pretty sure that my children's teachers and employers will tolerate them if they fit school and workplace norms; my chief worries about them do not concern others' attitudes toward their race.

23. I can criticize our government and talk about how much I fear its policies and behavior without being seen as a cultural outsider.

24. I can be pretty sure that if I ask to talk to the "person in charge," I will be facing a person of my race.

26. I can easily buy posters, post-cards, picture books, greeting cards, dolls, toys and children's magazines featuring people of my race.

27. I can go home from most meetings of organizations I belong to feeling somewhat tied in, rather than isolated, out-of-place, outnumbered, unheard, held at a distance or feared.

32. My culture gives me little fear about ignoring the perspectives and powers of people of other races.

46. I can choose blemish cover or bandages in "flesh" color and have them more or less match my skin.

All of these "privileges" are simply aspects of having a homogeneous homeland, of belonging to a community of people with whom you share a common biological and cultural heritage. In white societies, one can call this "white privilege." But in Asian societies, one would call it "Asian privilege" and in African societies, "African privilege." Furthermore, it is too crude to speak about privilege simply in terms of broad racial categories. Instead, we should speak about Norwegian privilege in Norway, Japanese privilege in Japan, Swazi privilege in Swaziland, and the like. It would also be nice to live in a world in which stateless peoples, like Palestinians and Kurds, have similar privileges.

McIntosh describes privilege as "invisible" and "weightless." We are "oblivious" of privilege. The unconscious aspect of privilege is also an aspect of having a homeland. A homeland is not just a realm in space. It is also a realm of meaning. To be truly at home, one must fully internalize and master these codes of meaning—language and manners being the most important—so one does not have to consciously reflect on them. Then one can simply relax and *live* rather than be self-conscious.

A foreign land is not just a place with unfamiliar people and things. The conventions are unfamiliar as well, thus one is constantly forced to reflect upon things that are taken for granted by the natives. Is this the right word? Is this the right greeting? How do I call 911?

It is fun to visit foreign lands, but it can be alienating, stressful, and psychologically exhausting to actually live in one, and this is the everyday experience of minorities and stateless peoples in other people's homelands. The cure to this problem is to give every people a land of their own where they can feel at home rather than constantly alienated.

Many of McIntosh's alleged privileges of being white are more accurately described as *the absence of the disadvantages of being black*. These include:

3. If I should need to move, I can be pretty sure of

renting or purchasing housing in an area which I can afford and in which I would want to live.

4. I can be pretty sure that my neighbors in such a location will be neutral or pleasant to me.

5. I can go shopping alone most of the time, pretty well assured that I will not be followed or harassed.

13. Whether I use checks, credit cards or cash, I can count on my skin color not to work against the appearance of financial reliability.

18. I can swear, or dress in second hand clothes, or not answer letters, without having people attribute these choices to the bad morals, the poverty or the illiteracy of my race.

19. I can speak in public to a powerful male group without putting my race on trial.

25. If a traffic cop pulls me over or if the IRS audits my tax return, I can be sure I haven't been singled out because of my race.

35. I can take a job with an affirmative action employer without having my co-workers on the job suspect that I got it because of my race.

36. If my day, week or year is going badly, I need not ask of each negative episode or situation whether it had racial overtones.

38. I can think over many options, social, political, imaginative or professional, without asking whether a person of my race would be accepted or allowed to

do what I want to do.

39. I can be late to a meeting without having the lateness reflect on my race.

40. I can choose public accommodation without fearing that people of my race cannot get in or will be mistreated in the places I have chosen.

41. I can be sure that if I need legal or medical help, my race will not work against me.

43. If I have low credibility as a leader I can be sure that my race is not the problem.

McIntosh describes black disadvantages as white privileges because she wishes to absolve blacks for these problems and blame whites. Unfortunately, many anti-black stereotypes—for instance, black criminality and financial irresponsibility—are not just dreamed up by evil-minded white people. They are based in experience.

Of course most blacks are not criminals and spendthrifts, but enough of them are that it is rational for whites to be vigilant around blacks they do not know, a burden of suspicion that falls equally upon the problem minority and the blameless majority.

It really is an injustice. But it is also rational, and whites should not feel guilty about it. Such rational distrust is an inevitable product of diversity, and it will only increase as our societies become more multicultural. The Left's only response to the rational distrust generated by diversity is to morally shame whites into dropping their guard, making them more vulnerable to predators and parasites.

One of the central contentions of the Black Lives Matter movement is that blacks are arrested for crimes at a greater rate than whites simply because of white racism. But objective data show that *blacks are arrested for crimes at pretty much the same rate that they commit them*.[4] Thus, if Black Lives Matter wishes to lower the black arrest rate, they should work to lower the black crime rate.

But there is not a single politician in America who has the courage to simply tell blacks to commit fewer crimes. Instead, police departments are being intimidated into giving blacks license to break the law with impunity. Police are also more likely to use violence with white suspects than blacks in comparable situations. This is objectively a system of black privilege.[5]

Blacks feel oppressed in white societies by negative white stereotypes. But the most momentous of these stereotypes are based in experience. Thus it is rational to use them as guides in dealing with black strangers. Because of this, no amount of reeducation is going to banish them.[6]

As long as multiracial societies persist, whites will continue to resent blacks for not living up to white standards, and blacks will continue to resent whites for imposing alien standards. The ethnonationalist solution to such irreconcilable differences is racial divorce: the creation of homogeneous sovereign homelands, to the extent that this is possible, for all distinct peoples who wish to exercise this right.

---

[4] See for instance, Edwin S. Rubenstein's *The Color of Crime: Race, Crime, and Justice in America* (Oakton, Vir.: New Century Foundation, 2016).

[5] On Black Lives Matter and the collapse of policing blacks, see Heather MacDonald's many studies on "the Ferguson effect." On the over-policing of whites in America, including increased chances of death by cop, see Richard Houck's "Law Enforcement and the Hostile Elite," *Counter-Currents*, June 20, 2018.

[6] For a more detailed discussion of the rationality of experience-based prejudices, see my essay "In Defense of Prejudice," in this volume.

The main reason to reject the claim that America is a white supremacist society is the fact that some non-white groups—chiefly East Asians and certain communities of South Asians—do better than whites in key indicators of success, such as educational attainment, income, and law abidingness, and they did so before anti-white discrimination and non-white tokenism became rampant. If American whites were intent on creating systematic white privilege and supremacy, we failed miserably. Therefore, white racism is not a sufficient explanation for differing racial outcomes in America.

We have an alternative hypothesis based on the science of Human Biological Diversity. The differing levels of education, income, and law-abidingness—to name just three factors—among racial groups in America are precisely what we would predict given measurable differences of IQ and sociopathic personality traits between the races. For a survey of the effect of IQ on a wide range of social outcomes, see Richard Lynn's *The Global Bell Curve*. On racial differences in personality traits beyond just IQ, including psychopathy, see Michael Levin's *Why Race Matters*.[7]

This does not mean that the American system is "fair" in the sense of being a color-blind meritocracy. We are perfectly willing to admit that some forms of discrimination favor whites—if it is also acknowledged that significant non-white privileges exist. But I believe that Human Biological Diversity is so powerful a determinant of social outcomes that it can basically overpower both white and anti-white privileges, allowing us to act *as if* these forces do not exist, even though we know that they do. In a similar way, although we know that other measurable psychological traits matter to social outcomes, IQ differences

---

[7] Michael Levin's *Why Race Matters* (Oakton, Vir.: New Century Books, 2016).

alone are so powerful at predicting social outcomes that we can act *as if* other factors do not exist. (This was brought home to me by Lynn's *The Global Bell Curve*.)

Different races really are different. That means that when different races live in the same social system, subject to the same laws, institutions, and incentives, some will inevitably flourish better than others. There will never be a social system that is equally conducive to the flourishing of all races and cultures. Such inequalities will persist even if we institute remedial forms of discrimination in favor of groups who lag behind. The science of Human Biological Diversity also explains why some non-white groups excel in white societies, even though they too have trouble finding flesh-colored band-aids.

Many of us would prefer not to mention biological racial differences at all, for fear of hurting the feelings of disadvantaged groups. But we have to talk about such differences, because the present system blames whites for the failure of some non-whites to flourish in white societies. As long as whites are charged with evil intentions to keep some races down, and as long as white institutions and ways of life are targeted for demolition and reconstruction by egalitarian social engineers, we must press the alternative hypothesis of biologically based inequality.

So if the different races are biologically unequal, what does this imply for social policy? Today's conservatives and libertarians think they can retain multiculturalism by establishing a true "color-blind" meritocracy. While I am all for meritocracy, it is simply naïve to believe that groups that will naturally gravitate toward the bottom of such a system—the "losers"—will be satisfied with their lot, even if they arrived there by entirely "fair" procedures, and even if they enjoy higher material standards of living than they could in non-white homelands.

Classical liberalism is simply blind to non-material motivations like honor and pride. Many non-whites would rather rule in hell (their own homelands) than serve in heaven (classical liberal meritocracies). Ethnonationalists, however, understand completely.

Every human being deserves a home, where he can be himself free of the interference of others. But we should feel at home outside our front doors as well. We should be able to live among people who share our language and values, our history and destiny, the whole litany of "white privileges." We don't just need homes. We need homelands. Not alienating, bewildering, multicultural bazaars filled with people who do not share our language and values. A country's Gross Domestic Product does not matter if nobody feels at home.

If races really are different, that means they will create different social systems. These systems will express their natures. They will feel as comfortable to them as well-fitting shoes. But this means that other races will not feel comfortable, even if they are treated with utmost courtesy and fairness—even if they are given advantages over the natives. The solution is not to further change our societies, to further abandon our norms and ways of life to accommodate outsiders. That simply doesn't work. Multiculturalism does not create societies where everyone feels at home. It creates societies where no one feels at home.

There is no moral imperative to destroy our homelands to accommodate strangers. There would be no such imperative even if it were possible. And there is certainly no imperative to destroy real homelands in pursuit of the impossible dream of a society in which all peoples feel equally at home.

But there is one place where all the peoples of the world can feel at home. It is called the planet earth. This planet is big enough for all races and nations to have places they can call their own. This is the ethnonationalist version of utopia. Privilege is inherently unequal. But everyone can be privileged in his own homeland. Norwegians can be privileged in Norway. Somalis can be privileged in Somalia. Kurds can be privileged in Kurdistan. As long as every people has a place to call home, there is nothing unfair about this situation.

Peggy McIntosh describes white privilege as a package of "unearned assets." That is meant as a criticism. But we must be careful here. Only a bourgeois individualist equates the unearned with the unjust. There are some cases where we have a right to unearned assets. For instance, if a gift truly is a gift, and not simply a disguised form of exchange, then it is an unearned asset to which we have a right. A gift created by past generations and handed on to future generations cannot be a disguised exchange, for there is no way to pay our ancestors back for our genetic and cultural heritage. We can only pay it forward, to future generations. A homeland is an unearned asset, a privilege, and you have every right to defend it zealously.

Norway is not something that all people can enjoy. It is something for yourselves and your posterity. It was created by your ancestors, carved out of a remarkably harsh environment through will and ingenuity. It was passed on to you, for safekeeping and improvement. And I hope you will pass it along to future generations once strangers like me have left your shores.

TECHNOLOGICAL UTOPIANISM &
ETHNIC NATIONALISM

The idea of creating a utopian society through scientific and technological progress goes back to such founders of modern philosophy as Bacon and Descartes, although the idea was already hinted at by Machiavelli. But today, most people's visions of technological utopia are derived from science fiction. With the notable exception of Frank Herbert's *Dune* series,[1] science fiction tends to identify progress with political liberalism and globalism. Just think of *Star Trek*, in which the liberal, multi-racial Federation is constantly battling against perennial evils like nationalism and eugenics. Thus it is worth asking: Is ethnic nationalism—which is illiberal and anti-globalist—compatible with technological utopianism or not?

My view is that technological utopianism is not only *compatible* with ethnic nationalism but also that *liberalism and globalization undermine technological progress*, and that *the ethnostate is actually the ideal incubator for mankind's technological apotheosis*.

Before arguing these points, however, I need to say a bit about what technological utopianism entails and why people think it is a natural fit with globalization. The word *utopia* literally means *nowhere* and designates a society that cannot be realized. But the progress of science and technology are all about *the conquest of nature*, i.e., the expansion of man's power and reach, so that utopia becomes attainable. Specific ambitions of scientific utopianism include the abolition of material scarcity, the exploration and settlement of the galaxy, the pro-

---

[1] Greg Johnson, "Archaeofuturist Fiction: Frank Herbert's *Dune*," *Counter-Currents*, August 15, 2014.

longation of human life, and the upward evolution of the human species.

It is natural to think that scientific and technological progress go hand in hand with globalization. Reality is one, therefore the science that understands reality and the technology that manipulates it must be one as well. Science and technology speak a universal language. They are cumulative collaborative enterprises that can mobilize the contributions of the best people from across the globe. So it seems reasonable that the road to technological utopia can only be impeded by national borders. I shall offer three arguments why this is not so.

1. GLOBALIZATION VS. INNOVATION

I define globalization as breaking down barriers to sameness: the same market, the same culture, the same form of government, the same way of life—what Alexandre Kojève called the "universal homogeneous state."

As Peter Thiel argues persuasively in *Zero to One*, globalization and technological innovation are actually two very different modes of progress.[2] Technological innovation creates something new. Globalization merely copies new things and spreads them around. Thiel argues, furthermore, that globalization without technological innovation is not sustainable. For instance, it is simply not possible for China and India to consume as much fossil fuel as the First World countries, but that is entailed by globalization within the present technological context. In the short run, this sort of globalization will have catastrophic environmental effects. In the long run, it will hasten the day when our present form of civilization collapses when fossil fuels are exhausted. To stave off this apocalypse, we need new innovations, par-

---

[2] Peter Thiel, *Zero to One: Notes on Startups, or How to Build the Future* (New York: Crown, 2014).

ticularly in the area of energy.

The most important technological innovations of the 20th century are arguably splitting the atom and the conquest of space. Neither was accomplished by private enterprise spurred by consumer demand in a global liberal-democratic society. Instead, they were created by rival governments locked in hot and cold warfare: first the United States and its Allies against the Axis powers in World War II, then the United States and the capitalist West versus the Soviet Bloc until the collapse of Communism in 1989–1991.

Indeed, one can argue that the rivalry between capitalism and communism began to lose its technological dynamism because of the statesmanship of Richard Nixon, who began détente with the USSR with the Strategic Arms Limitations Talks in 1969, then went to China in 1971, lessening the threat that the Communist powers would recoalesce into a single bloc. Détente ended with the Soviet invasion of Afghanistan in 1979. Ronald Reagan's Strategic Defense Initiative could have spurred major technological advances, but merely threatening it was enough to persuade Gorbachev to seek a political solution. So the ideal situation for spurring technological growth is *political rivalry without political resolution*, thereby necessitating immense expenditures on research and development to gain technological advantages.

Since the collapse of Communism and the rise of a unipolar liberal-democratic world order, however, the driving force of technological change has been consumer demand. Atomic energy and sending men into space have been pretty much abandoned, and technological progress has been primarily channeled into information technology, which has made some of us more productive but for the most part just allows us to amuse ourselves with smartphones as society declines around us.

But we are not going to be able to Tweet ourselves out

of looming environmental crises and Malthusian traps. Only fundamental innovations in energy technology will do the trick. And only the state, which can command enormous resources and unite a society around a common purpose, has a record of accomplishment in this area.

Of course none of the parties to the great conflicts that spurred technological growth were ethnonationalists in the strict sense, not even the Axis powers. Indeed, liberal democracy and communism were merely rival visions of global society. But when rival visions of globalization are slugging it out for power, that means that the globe is divided among a plurality of different political actors.

Pluralism and rivalry have spurred states to the greatest technological advances in history. Globalization, pacification, and liberalism have not only halted progress but have bred complacency in the face of potential global disasters. A global marketplace will never take mankind to the stars. It will simply distract us until civilization collapses and the Earth becomes a scorched boneyard.

2. INNOVATION VS. COST-CUTTING

In economics, productivity is defined as a mathematical formula: outputs divided by inputs, i.e., the cost per widget. Mathematically speaking, you can increase productivity either by making labor more productive, chiefly through technological innovation, or simply by cutting costs.

Most of the productivity gains that come from economic globalization are a matter of cost-cutting, primarily cutting the costs of labor. The Third World has a vast supply of cheap labor. Economic globalization allows the free movement of labor and capital. Businesses can cut labor costs by moving factories overseas or by importing new workers to drive down wages at home.

Historically speaking, the greatest economic spur to technological innovation has been high labor costs. The way to raise labor costs is to end economic globalization,[3] by cutting off immigration and by putting high tariffs on foreign manufactured goods. In short, we need economic nationalism. Indeed, only economic nationalism can lead to a post-scarcity economy.

What exactly is a "post-scarcity economy," and how can we get there from here? First of all, not all forms of scarcity can be abolished. Unique and handcrafted items will always be scarce. There will only be one *Mona Lisa*. Scarcity can only be abolished with identical, mass-produced items. Second, the cost of these items will only approach zero in terms of labor. Basically, we will arrive at a post-scarcity economy when machines put everyone involved in mass production out of work. But the machines, raw materials, and energy used in production will still have some costs. Thus the post-scarcity economy will arrive through innovation in robotics and energy production. The best image of a post-scarcity world is the "replicator" in *Star Trek*, which can change the atomic structure of basic inputs to materialize things out of thin air.

Of course workers who are replaced by machines can't be allowed to starve. The products of machines have to be consumed by someone. Production can be automated, but consumption cannot. It would be an absurdist dystopia if mechanization led to the starvation of workers, so consumption had to be automated as well. One set of robots would produce things, then another set of robots would consume them and add zeroes to the bank balances of a few lonely plutocrats.

To make the post-scarcity economy work, we need to

---

[3] Greg Johnson, "The End of Globalization," in *Truth, Justice, & a Nice White Country*.

ensure that people can afford to buy its products. There are two basic ways this can be done.

First, the productivity gains of capital have to be shared with the workers, through rising wages or shrinking work weeks. When workers are eliminated entirely, they need to receive generous pensions.

Second, every economic system requires a medium of exchange. Under the present system, the state gives private banks the ability to create money and charge interest on its use. The state also provides a whole range of direct payments to individuals: welfare, old-age pensions, etc. A *universal basic income* is a direct government payment to *all* citizens that is sufficient to ensure basic survival in a First World country.[4] Such an income would allow the state to ensure economic liquidity, so that every product has a buyer, while eliminating two very costly middlemen: banks and social welfare bureaucracies.

All of this sounds pretty far out. But it is only unattainable in the present globalized system, in which cost-cutting is turning high-tech, First World industrial economies into low-tech Third World cheap-labor plantation economies. Only economic nationalism can spur the technological innovations necessary to create a post-scarcity economy by raising labor costs, both through immigration controls and tariff walls against cheap foreign manufactured goods.

3. ETHNONATIONALISM & SCIENCE

So far we have established that scientific and technological progress are undermined by globalization and encouraged by nationalist economic policies and the rivalries between nations and civilizational blocs. But we

---

[4] Greg Johnson, "Money for Nothing," in *Truth, Justice, & a Nice White Country*.

need a more specific argument to establish that ethnonationalism is especially in harmony with scientific and technological progress.

My first premise is: *No form of government is fully compatible with scientific and technological progress if it is founded on dogmas that are contrary to fact.* For instance, the republic of Oceania might have a population of intelligent and industrious people, an excellent educational system, first rate infrastructure, and a booming economy. But if the state religion of Oceania mandates that the Earth is flat and lies at the center of the universe, Oceania is not going to take us to the stars.

My second premise is: *The advocacy of racially and ethnically diverse societies—regardless of whether they have liberal or conservative regimes—is premised on the denial of political experience and the science of human biological diversity.*

The history of human societies offers abundant evidence that putting multiple ethnic groups under the same political system is a recipe for otherwise avoidable ethnic tensions and conflicts. Furthermore, science indicates that the most important factors for scientific and technological advancement—intelligence and creativity—are primarily genetic, and they are not equally distributed among the races. Finally, Genetic Similarity Theory predicts that the most harmonious and happy societies will be the most genetically homogeneous, with social conflict increasing with genetic diversity.

Denying these facts is anti-scientific in two ways. First and most obviously, it is simply the refusal to look at objective facts that contradict the dogma that diversity improves society. Second, basing a society on this dogma undermines the genetic and social conditions necessary for progress and innovation, for instance by lowering the average IQ and creating greater social conflict. Other things being equal, these factors will make a society less likely to foster scientific and technological innovation.

My third premise is: *Ethnonationalism is based on both political experience and the science of human biological diversity—and does not deny any other facts.* Therefore, *ethnonationalism is more compatible with scientific and technological progress than are racially and ethnically diverse societies—other things being equal.*

Of course some research and development projects require so much money and expertise that they can only be undertaken by large countries like the United States, China, India, or Russia. Although we can predict with confidence that all of these societies would improve their research and development records if they were more racially and culturally homogeneous, even in their present states they can accomplish things that small, homogeneous ethnostates simply cannot dream of.

For instance, if a country of two million people like Slovenia were to adopt ethnonationalism, it would probably outperform a more diverse society with the same size and resources in research and development. But it would not be able to colonize Mars. However, just as small countries can defend themselves from big countries by creating alliances, small states can work together on scientific and technological projects too big to undertake on their own. But no alliance is stronger than its weakest member. Since diversity is a weakness and homogeneity is a strength, we can predict that cooperative research and development efforts among ethnostates will probably be more fruitful than those among diverse societies.

Now someone might object that one can improve upon the ethnostate by taking in only high-IQ immigrants from other races. Somehow Americans went to the Moon without importing Asians and Indians. Such people are being imported today for two reasons. First, importing foreign brains allows us to evade problems with producing our own, namely, dysgenic fertility and the collapse of American STEM education, largely due to political correctness, i.e., racial integration and the denial of biological intelligence differences. Second, the productivity gains attributed to diversity in technology are simply due to cost-cutting. But the real answer is: The Internet allows whites to collaborate with the best scientists around the world. So we don't need to live with them.

To sum up: The idea that technological utopia will go hand-in-hand with the emergence of a global homogeneous society is false. The greatest advances in technology were spurred by the rivalries of hostile political powers, and with the emergence of a unipolar world, technological development has been flagging.

The idea that technological utopia goes hand-in-hand with liberal democracy is false. Liberalism from its very inception has been opposed to the idea that there is a common good of society. Liberalism is all about empowering individuals to pursue private aims and advantages. It denies that the common good exists; or, if the common good exists, liberalism denies that it is knowable; or if the common good exists and is knowable, liberalism denies that it can be pursued by the state, but instead will be brought about by an invisible hand if we just allow private individuals to go about their business.

The only thing that can bring liberal democrats together to pursue great common aims is the threat of war. This is what sent Americans to the Moon. America's greatest technological achievements were fostered by the government, not private enterprise, and in times of hot and cold war, not peace. Since the end of the Cold War, however, victory has defeated us. America is no longer a serious country.

The solution, though, is not to go back to war, but to junk liberalism and return to the classical idea that there is a common good that can and must be pursued by the state. A liberal democracy can only be a serious country if someone like the Russians threatens to nuke them every minute of the day. Normal men and normal societies pursue the common good, because once one is convinced something really is good, one needs no additional reason to pursue it. But if you need some extra incentives, consider the environmental devastation and civilizational collapse that await us as the fossil fuel economy continues to expand like an algae bloom to its global limits. That should concentrate the mind wonderfully.

The idea that technological utopia will go hand-in-hand with global capitalism is false. Globalization has undermined technological innovation by allowing businesses to raise profits merely by cutting costs. The greatest advances in manufacturing technology have been spurred by high labor costs, which are products of a strong labor movement, closed borders, and protectionism.

Finally, the idea that technological utopianism will go hand-in-hand with racially and ethnically diverse societies is false. This is where ethnonationalism proves its superiority. Diversity promotes social conflict and removes barriers to dysgenic breeding. The global average IQ is too low to create a technological utopia. Global race-mixing will make Europeans more like the global average. Therefore, it will extinguish all dreams of progress. Ethnonationalists, however, are actually willing to replace dysgenic reproductive trends with eugenic ones, to ensure that every future generation has more geniuses, including scientific ones. And if you need an extra incentive, consider the fact that China is pursuing eugenics while in the West it is fashionable to adopt Haitian babies. Ethnonationalism, moreover, promotes social harmony and cohesion, which make possible coordinated efforts toward common goals.

What sort of society will conquer scarcity, conquer

death, and settle the cosmos? A society that practices economic nationalism to encourage automation. A homogeneous, high-IQ society with eugenic rather than dysgenic reproductive trends. A harmonious, cohesive, high-trust society that can work together on common projects. An illiberal society that is willing to mobilize its people and resources to achieve great common aims. In short, if liberal democracy and global capitalism are returning us to the mud, it is ethnonationalism that will take us to the stars.

FREEDOM OF SPEECH

I've got good news and bad news.

The good news is that everyone likes to get good news. It is easy to bring good news and easy to receive it.

The bad news is that nobody likes to get bad news. It is hard to bring bad news and hard to receive it. Receiving bad news is upsetting, which is why bringing bad news is difficult. Sometimes one has to deal with tears and anger.

But bad news is always more important than good news, because if something is going wrong you need to know. Bad news is not a problem. Bad news is one's *awareness* of a problem. And no matter how bad a problem is, it is usually better to know than not know, because knowing about a problem is the first step towards fixing it. The only situation in which it might be better not to know is if a problem is insoluble, so that knowing about it simply adds to the problem rather than helps alleviate it.

Because bad news is upsetting, people often respond to it irrationally. Sometimes they would prefer not to know, even though you can't solve problems you don't know about. Sometimes they misplace their emotions. Instead of getting upset with the problem itself and seeking to solve it, they get upset with the bad news and seek to punish the bearer. But this is foolish, because society works best when information flows freely, and the most important information is bad news.

Because receiving bad news is upsetting and giving it is risky, dealing with bad news is a test of character. Those who receive bad news have to master their emotions, for if you dissolve into tears or explode into anger, you are making it more burdensome to bring you bad

news in the future, which means that you might not receive news about a problem until it is too late to rectify
it. Bringing bad news is also a test of character, because
one always risks unpleasant personal consequences, but
sometimes short-run personal risks are necessary to secure the greater good in the long run. But since the bearers of bad news are doing us all a favor, it is incumbent
upon us to reduce the risks to the absolute minimum.
This is why freedom of speech needs to be a right en-
shrined in the fundamental law of every land.

One does not need the right to freedom of speech to
tell people what they want to hear. Freedom of speech is
the freedom to tell people what they don't want to
hear—but need to hear anyway. A right to freedom of
speech, moreover, is not necessary when one bears bad
news to powerless people, for instance one's children,
one's students, or one's employees. After all, they can't
punish you for your good deed. We need the *right* to
freedom of speech when we bear bad news to people
who are more powerful than us—people who need bad
news to make important decisions, and people who have
the power to punish the bearers of bad news. But they
can't punish us if free speech is our right. Our rights
trump their anger.

The two most important things for White Nationalists
today are:

First, breaking down the taboo against white identity
politics, i.e., the idea that it is *immoral* for whites—and
only whites—to take our own side in ethnic conflicts.

Second, maintaining our freedom of speech long
enough to destroy that taboo.

White Nationalists are the bearers of bad news: that
diversity is not a strength, but a source of alienation,
conflict, and violence; that modern politics and morals
have put our race on a path to extinction; and the only
solution is to abandon liberalism, hedonistic individual-

ism, globalization, and multiculturalism and bring back healthier, pro-white policies and values. We are changing people's minds, and the establishment is powerless to change them back. Thus they are trying to censor us.

How can we deal with this threat?

In the short run, we need an internet Bill of Rights to protect dissidents from censorship and deplatforming. Beyond that, we need an across-the-board ban on politically-correct terms of service and employment, so we are free to dissent without threatening our livelihoods and social capital. If we can get such legislation in place, I am confident that we can win, and sooner rather than later. We will change so many minds that we will reach a tipping point. The taboo against white identity politics will melt away. Pro-white values will pervade the culture. Eventually we can mobilize enough support to overthrow the existing political establishment and replace it with a pro-white one.

But who told us that this would be safe and easy? White Nationalists are battling against the most all-encompassing soft-totalitarian system in history. It is a system bent on nothing short of the genocide of the white race, a goal so evil that when Plato and Aristotle drew up their lists of bad regimes, it was simply inconceivable. To overthrow this system, we might have to risk much more than our livelihoods. We might have to risk our very lives.

In the long run, though, we are probably going to win even if we don't get an internet Bill of Rights. Censorship can slow us down, but it can't really stop us. Already people are laying the foundations for a new internet that will be free of the choke points where censors perch. Thus, ultimately, the only way to prevent us from getting our message out online will be to shut down the web entirely. But the establishment cannot contemplate that, because the global political and economic system depends on the Internet.

The establishment—or at least the tiny stratum that is fully aware of the present threat of white identity politics—has the same relationship to the Internet as a junkie to his habit. He knows that it will kill him in the long run. But very few junkies overcome their addiction because they cannot bear the short-term pain, even if it is the price of long-term survival.

Human beings might best be defined as the intermittently rational animal, and one of the most pervasive forms of irrationality is pursuing short-term self-indulgence at the expense of long-term well-being. This is how nations and individuals get into debt; this is how economic, demographic, and ecological crises arise. Fortunately for us, it is also how the system will fail to do the only thing that can stop the rise of White Nationalism—until it is too late.

So be of good cheer. If we continue to get our message out, we will win. And internet censorship cannot stop that process. It can only make it slower and more difficult.

Once we win, what should our attitude be toward free speech? Some White Nationalists see free speech as merely a means to take power. I wish to argue that free speech is something that we will want to keep after we win.

Freedom of speech is a value because we are all *fallible* and *vulnerable*. Fallibility means that we can make mistakes. We can have false or inadequate pictures of the world that can be improved upon. Vulnerability simply means that unforeseeable contingencies can upset our best laid plans. To overcome mistakes and misfortunes, we first need to know about them. That means that we need the freedom to be the bearers of bad news. We need freedom of speech, because it makes genuine intellectual and social progress possible.

A society that lacks the ability to change lacks the ability to preserve itself. But a society can't change if it lacks the ability to communicate bad news to its leaders. This is why we should want to protect freedom of speech, even when we are the ones in power.

Why do people oppose freedom of speech? There are two main reasons.

First, some people think they *already* have the truth. This truth is, moreover, absolute: It is complete and not subject to revision. Any contrary position is, therefore, a falsehood. This is why religions in the Abrahamic tradition—including Marxism—have opposed freedom of speech. They claim to be absolutely true. Therefore, all other religions are false—or, at best, semblances of the truth—and must be suppressed.

Second, people with a vested interest in a given political and economic system don't like criticism because it threatens their power and peace of mind.

Both views are irrational.

We all make mistakes. We all suffer misfortunes. But only some of us are destroyed by them. Others learn from them and overcome them. But, again, the first step to overcoming a problem is knowing that one has it.

One of the most powerful ideas of Plato's *Republic* is that political regimes and personality types have analogous structures, so the city can throw light on the soul, and the soul can throw light on the city.

Years ago, I read a listicle on signs that your boss might be a narcissist. The item that made the strongest impression on me is that narcissists tend to punish bearers of bad news.

Defining narcissism is a tricky thing, because we live in a society in which all manifestations of honor, especially male honor, have been pathologized as narcissism. There is nothing wrong with thinking well of yourself and demanding that others treat you with respect. There is nothing wrong with taking pleasure in praise for your achievements. There is nothing wrong with high self-esteem, as long as it is based on objective merits.

Narcissism is a problem, though, when one puts *preserving a positive self-image* ahead of *positive self-actualization.*

Everyone makes mistakes. The path to self-actualization requires that we acknowledge our mistakes, take responsibility for them, learn what we can from them, and then rise above them. The narcissist, however, seeks to preserve his positive self-image at all costs. So when confronted with his mistakes, he denies them and doubles down on them. Or he blames others for his mistakes. Or he goes on the attack, particularly against the bearer of bad news. Anything, really, to avoid taking responsibility and acknowledging that he might have some room to learn and grow.

Narcissists may be highly attractive people. They may have enormous potential. Unfortunately, they think they are perfect just the way they are, and such complacency is deadly to personal growth. So as time passes, you will notice that narcissists seldom actualize their potential. Instead, they come off as dilettantes with a smooth patter. Older narcissists also seem increasingly puerile when compared to their contemporaries.

Narcissists, moreover, have difficulty maintaining friendships. Friends tell you what you *need* to hear—even if it is painful. Flatterers tell you what you *want* to hear. Friends aid self-actualization because they will tell you bad news. Flatterers encourage complacency because they only tell you how wonderful you are. Friends threaten a narcissist's positive self-image, whereas flatterers reinforce it.

Obviously it is disastrous to put narcissists into positions of power, because they end up making important decisions based on false or incomplete information fed to them by flatterers. It is no way to run a society.

Today's censorious establishment is narcissism writ large.

By censoring and suppressing White Nationalist ideas, the establishment changes almost nothing. We like to flatter ourselves that the White Nationalist movement is the driving force behind the rise of white racial consciousness. Our enemies share the same illusion. But the main forces behind the rise of White Nationalism are the moral outrages and catastrophic consequences of multiculturalism and white dispossession. People are coming to us in droves less because our movement is *pulling* them than because the system is *pushing* them. Which means that white racial consciousness will continue to rise even if White Nationalists are completely silenced.

Our anti-white oppressors, of course, do not see it that way, for that would threaten their positive self-image. The rise of white identity politics cannot be their fault. So it has to be our fault. They think white identity politics only exists because silver-tongued deceivers like Jared Taylor and Millennial Woes have Twitter accounts. Which is why they conclude that censorship will actually stop us. But White Nationalists are not the cause of ethnic conflict. We are just the bearers of bad news—and advocates of a workable alternative.

Censoring White Nationalists online does not stop people from noticing things, drawing conclusions, and formulating dissenting thoughts. It does not prevent people from discretely communicating their thoughts face to face or organizing in the real world. All censorship does is render the full extent of dissent invisible. This makes it difficult for the establishment to make rational political decisions. Censorship does not make the system stronger; it only makes it blinder, brittler, and more vulnerable. Advocates of censorship are like people who remove the battery from their smoke detector because they are tired of false alarms. But when the house catches fire, you need to know sooner than later.

If I were running a society, I would like to know who the dissidents are and what they think. Thus I would make freedom of speech a fundamental political right. If the dissidents are right, we can learn from them. If they are wrong, we can instruct them. If they are dangerously and stubbornly wrong, we can keep an eye on them.

But if we win, are we really going to give our enemies the freedom to regroup and rebrand, then lead our people back down the road to extinction once more? Don't we want to shut their dirty, lying mouths forever?

There are two points here.

First, if we do come to power, we will have to purge the existing institutions. We will not leave wealth, influence, and political power in the hands of implacable enemies. We will take away their platforms in politics, the media, and the academy. We will just give them early retirements and a lifetime ban on addressing the public. Then we will fill their positions with people who are loyal to us. But that is a far cry from instituting a regime of intellectual censorship.

Second, even if there is a great purge of the existing system, no matter what kind of society you have, in every generation, there will be aberrant personalities who are drawn to ideas that threaten social order. The best way of preventing bad ideas and institutional subversion from taking root again is not to create a world where people have never heard of such things. Instead, we need to create a world where *everyone* has heard of them. A proper education imparts sound information as well as healthy values and tastes. Such an education will inoculate us against bad ideas. We don't have to censor bad ideas if we are immune to them.

Evil will always be with us. But we need not fear it if we are immune to its charms. We should keep evil around, but keep it powerless, as a kind of *memento mo-ri*, a death's head at the feast, so we have a constant reminder of the hell on earth we will vanquish—but only if we start using, and defending, our freedom of speech today.

IN DEFENSE OF PREJUDICE

Years ago, a friend told me a parable about a species of hominid that did not live to inherit the earth. These hominids regarded each and every entity as entirely unique. When a tiger leaped out of the darkness and dragged one of them to his doom, this did not prompt any generalizations about tigers as a group. Thus when a new tiger began to prowl the shadows at the verge of the firelight, he was not judged on the basis of the other tiger's behavior. Indeed, if the first tiger came back, they would not have judged him on the basis of his past behavior either, because that was then, and this is now: two unique, individual moments in time.

But even though tigers are not always man-eaters, and man-eaters are not always hungry, these poor creatures still went extinct, because their problems were not limited to tigers. They could not learn from any experiences at all. They were just too dumb to survive.

Survival, you see, requires the ability to learn from past experiences so that one can *predict* and even *control* future ones. To do this, however, one must recognize that there are not just *individual* beings, but *kinds* or *types* of beings. Individuals belong to the same kind if they share a common nature. And, since what we can do follows from our nature, we can infer that if a tiger is dangerous once, it will probably be dangerous again. And if one tiger is dangerous, it is probable that other tigers are dangerous too. Thus if one of us is killed by a tiger, we can take reasonable precautions to make sure that it does not happen again.

Drawing conclusions about kinds based on individuals is called *inductive generalization*. Induction allows you to infer that all members of a kind are "like that" based on one's experience of individual members. These purple berries made me sick today, so they will probably make me sick tomorrow, since their nature and mine will probably not change overnight. And since you have the same nature as me, they might make you sick too. And since the purple berries on this bush are the same as the ones on the first bush, they'll probably make us sick too. The flesh of this animal tastes good to me, so it will probably taste good to you too, since we have the same nature. And other members of its kind will probably taste good to us as well, since they have the same nature too.

However, induction also teaches that natural traits tend to graph along bell curves, with a large number of typical cases in the middle, and small numbers of atypical cases on each end. Typical purple berries will make us sick, but on every bush, there might be some that have no negative effect and others that are downright toxic. Thus, inductive generalizations hold "not always, but for the most part." In terms of any given trait, "Not all X are like that." But most of them are.

Inductive reasoning is, therefore, *probabilistic*. There is always the possibility that one is not dealing with a typical instance of a kind. But it is not likely, since the atypical is by definition rare. Furthermore, as we experience more particulars, it becomes less likely that we are dealing with outliers, and our generalizations about a type become increasingly fixed. We even come to have a sense of what outliers are typical.

Although this is not common parlance, one could refer to a well-established inductive generalization as a "stereotype," which comes from the Greek *stereos* (στερεός), "fixed" or "firm," and the Greek *typos* (τύπος), or "type."

Inductive generalization does not just allow us to learn from past experience, which would be of merely theoretical interest. Induction also has important *practical* implications, for it allows us to *predict* future experiences based on past ones, thus allowing us to act advantageously, even intervene in the course of events and control natural phenomena.

Another word for predicting future experiences is pre-judging them. Another word for a pre-judgment is a prejudice. Now, some prejudices may be utterly baseless and irrational—e.g., prejudices rooted in bad inductive generalizations, superstition, or mental illness—and acting on them may lead to disaster. But well-founded inductive generalizations (stereotypes) are the basis of well-founded prejudices that can be highly advantageous—for instance, helping us to discriminate between dangerous breeds and gentle ones, poisonous mushrooms and edible ones, etc.

Induction, by giving us the ability to predict future events, is the foundation of *practical reason*, which is the primary human means of survival. Induction is also the basis of *science* and *technology*, which allow us to more deeply understand nature and thus to predict and control her better. Induction is thus the foundation of the ongoing conquest of nature that we call modernization and progress.

Stereotypes and well-founded prejudices may be triumphs of inductive reasoning and the foundations of common sense, science, technology, and progress. But today, when it comes to judging human beings, we are told that stereotypes and prejudices are evil and that each individual should be judged on his own behavior, not on the basis of the past behaviors of his kind. We are told that it is an injustice to judge individuals based on group membership.

This viewpoint is a kind of perversion of individualism. I myself defend a kind of Aristotelian individualism. I hold that the purpose of life is the actualization of our individual potentialities for excellence. In terms of politics, a well-ordered society should encourage individual self-actualization and excellence, as long as it does not undermine the common good of society.

The perverse individualism I reject, however, has nothing to do with individual self-actualization. Indeed, it basically amounts to a moral imperative to be *stupid*, since it is an attack on inductive generalization as such, which is the foundation of practical reason, science, technology, and the modern world. Perverse individualism demands that we behave like the hypothetical hominids discussed above, which were simply too stupid to survive.

False individualism is really an applied form of *nominalism*, which is the theory that there are no natural kinds in the world, only individuals, and all concepts of kinds are merely social conventions or "constructs." According to false individualism, justice requires that we ignore all groups—except, somehow, "humanity"—and judge each individual as an individual, without any preconceptions based on his membership in any merely constructed category, such as race. Nominalism, however, is metaphysically false. There are real natural kinds. Individual members of those kinds share natural traits that allow us to make probabilistic predictions about them based on what we know of their kind.

An individualist could, however, reply that even though nominalism is metaphysically false and there are natural kinds, we should still set aside our well-founded stereotypes and prejudices and judge each and every human being as an individual. In effect, we have to treat every individual as a potential outlier, even though most of them are not. Why? Because, apparently, every individual is of infinite value, so rendering justice is an absolute value and committing injustice is an absolute evil. We must act as if nominalism is true, because otherwise there is a vanishingly small possibility that we might be unjust to a stranger.

This position is a moralistic absurdity, for it simply cannot be practiced. There are seven billion people on this planet. It is impossible to treat each and every one as a special snowflake, and if one tried it, even with the limited numbers of people we encounter in our individual lives, it would consume all one's time and make it impossible to pursue one's own goals, i.e., to actually live. Because the purpose of life is self-actualization, and the time we have is short, we just cannot get to know everyone we deal with.

One of the ways that civilization advances is by giving us means of dealing with greater numbers of people than we can ever know as individuals. The market economy, for instance, allows individuals to interact with millions of others around the globe through a largely anonymous symbolic medium that, at least in theory, allows all participants to pursue their individual self-actualization.

Psychologists have observed that the human mind cannot deal with more than 150 or so direct personal relationships, which means that if we could deal only with people as individuals, civilization would regress to the complexity of a hunter-gatherer band or agricultural village.

Well-founded stereotypes and prejudices make possible highly complex societies by allowing us to size up individuals at a glance and to choose to embrace or avoid them. Since natural kinds are limited in number, we actually create artificial kinds with visible distinctions—accents, clothing styles, even uniforms—that allow us to chart a course through complex social situations at a glance. For instance, a black man dressed in a ghetto clown costume signals danger, whereas a black man dressed in a police uniform signals trustworthiness.

Furthermore, if stereotyping is wrong, why do people go to great lengths to stereotype themselves? We all want to find like-minded people, and dressing in a certain way is one means to communicate the group we belong to, e.g., hipster, preppy, metal, redneck, businessman, career woman, slut, prole, gay clone, black thug, etc. Blacks go to great trouble and expense to dress like thugs, in order to communicate that they are dangerous, or that they aspire to be. Why do white liberals think it is disrespectful to take their signaling seriously?

The idea that we should always treat others only as individuals also undermines one of the greatest gifts of modernity: privacy. It is fashionable to bemoan the impersonal and mediated nature of modern society, but in a smaller scale, more personal society, everybody knows everybody else's business. Thus it can be liberating to live in a society in which most people only know you by the persona you project and the money that you spend. Years ago, a student of mine told me that she grew up in a small Georgia town full of prying, censorious Baptists. She said she could hardly wait to move to Atlanta. I'll never forget her reason why: "So I could sin."

Under what conditions do we want to be judged as special snowflakes? We all want a fair shake when we are applying for a job or are on trial for our lives. But even then, chances are we are trying to conceal as much as we reveal. Moreover, we know that employers often can look only at the most superficial criteria simply because they lack the time to dig deeper. But we hope that we can at least expect justice from the criminal justice system. Beyond that, when nothing really crucial is at stake, we are content to navigate with prejudices and stereotypes, i.e., to play the odds with others and accept that others do the same with us.

Since nobody can judge each and every person as an individual all the time, it stands to reason that people only trot out this imperative to use as a weapon against others. Universalists of both the Left and Right typically deploy it against any form of racism, nationalism, tribalism, or antipathy to various religious groups or categories of sexual deviants. Of course, if you prod these universalists just a little, you find that they have some rather poorly formed and emotionally charged stereotypes and prejudices about their opponents.

"Not all Xs are like that," the universalists say, implying that it is a mortal sin not to appreciate the uniqueness of every special snowflake. And since group membership can never be a basis for excluding someone from our society, there can be no racially and ethnically homogeneous societies, and we cannot uphold any norms of social and sexual behavior. Thus perverse individualism is just a tool to make us incapable of resisting ethnic dispossession and social decadence. What kind of people preach (but do not practice) "blindness" to race, ethnicity, religion, and sexual identity as a moral imperative? Obviously, people who are up to no good.

If you propose discrimination against pedophiles, you will be told that they aren't *all* child molesters, and you can't do anything against them until after they have been caught. If you propose discrimination against blacks or mestizos because of their propensity to criminality, you are told that they are not all like that, and we can't do anything against them until they actually commit crimes. If you propose discrimination against Muslims on the grounds that their religion mandates lies, rape, terrorism, murder, enslavement, and the overthrow of all governments, you will be told that not all Muslims are like that, and we can't do anything against them until after they have committed a crime. If you propose discrimination against Jews because they are a hostile elite working to corrupt our politics and culture and destroy our race by promoting white guilt, miscegenation, and race-replacement immigration, you will be told that they aren't all like that, and it would be collectivism to treat them simply as an enemy group. We have to treat all members of problem groups as if they are innocent, until proven otherwise. It is immoral to try to separate ourselves entirely from problem groups. Instead, we need to give them a chance, which boils down to a chance to harm us. And that means no borders and no standards.

These perverse individualists might even try to argue that the soldiers of an invading army are not all out to kill us, so it would be unjust to kill them just because they carry arms against us. But at that point, we would see what they really are and stand them against a wall. Of course by then it might be too late.

I am a nationalist because I believe that racial, ethnic, and religious diversity within the same political system are not strengths but weaknesses. They are constant sources of simmering tension that frequently boil over into hatred and violence. Thus the best guarantee of peace and harmony is to create separate homelands for all peoples. A healthy society also requires norms regarding sexuality, marriage, and child-rearing. Thus a society has to practice discrimination. We have to discriminate between who is us and who is not. And within our group, we have to discriminate between the normal and abnormal, the optimal and suboptimal, the law-abiding and the criminal.

We can freely acknowledge that there are some good blacks, Muslims, and Jews. There just aren't enough of them for our tastes. But even if these groups were equal or superior to us—and they are bound to be superior in some ways—in the end they are simply *not us*, and we wish to create societies for ourselves and our posterity. We are not creating a team for a sporting event or a spelling bee by recruiting exceptional outliers from a wide range of different groups. We seek to create homogeneous communities with full ranges of both average specimens and outliers, i.e., organic white communities, which are one in blood and culture but diverse in abilities, opinions, and interests, so that all of our people have places to call home.

WHY RACE IS NOT A
SOCIAL CONSTRUCT

Race realism is one of the intellectual foundations of White Nationalism. Race realism is the thesis that racial differences are *objective facts of nature*, which pre-exist human consciousness, human society, and even the human race itself—since there were different species and subspecies before mankind emerged.

Nature must be understood in contrast to *conventions*—like human languages and laws—which do not exist independent of human consciousness and society.

As objective facts of nature, racial differences cannot be safely ignored. Nor can natural racial differences be transformed simply by altering legal or linguistic conventions. Conventions can only alter racial realities by guiding human action to change nature itself. For instance, if we institute eugenic or dysgenic incentives, this will change the genes of future generations.

The opposite of race realism is the idea of the "social construction of race," the thesis that racial differences are not objective facts but rather shared social conventions, which may vary from time to time and from place to place, like languages and table manners.

The social construction of race is one of the intellectual foundations of racial egalitarianism, for if race is socially constructed, then so is racial inequality. This offers the possibility that racial inequality can be replaced with equality simply by altering social conventions, like laws and language.

THE BASIS OF RACE REALISM

The basis of race realism is sense experience. Different races *appear* different from one another. Different subraces appear different from one another. Racially mixed children appear different from pure specimens. Even races that appear superficially similar—like Australian aborigines and African blacks—appear to be different on closer inspection. Careful observers do not confuse the two. Racial differences are not just a matter of "skin color," but of morphology and behavior as well, all of which can be observed empirically.[1]

Note that I do not claim that racial realism is based in *science*. People were aware of racial differences long before the emergence of science. Science comes along only later, to explain observable racial differences. Scientific theories are, moreover, verified or falsified based on their ability to explain observed racial differences. Observable racial differences are, therefore, the Alpha and the Omega of racial science. Thus the foundation of race realism is sense experience, not scientific theorizing.

This is important to understand, because it implies that problems with theories of race do not in any way alter the perceptible differences between races.

It is also important to understand that race realism is the default, common-sense position of all mankind. We observe differences between races, subraces, and hybrids—human and otherwise—before we learn words to communicate and classify them, and before we create theories to explain them.

I vividly remember my first experience of a non-white: a waiter in the dining car of a train. I was 4 or 5 years old. I was especially taken by the contrast in color between

---

[1] An excellent basic textbook on race distinguished in terms of observable, morphological features which remains valid to this day is Carleton S. Coon, *The Living Races of Man* (New York: Random House, 1965). The book is particularly valuable for its many photographs illustrating typical racial, subracial, and hybrid types.

the back and the front of the man's hands. When he went away, I asked my mother what I had seen, and she told me that he was not just a white man turned brown, but a different kind of man called a "Negro." But I already *saw* the differences before I was *told* the name and explanation. Indeed, I asked for an explanation *because* I saw the differences. My mother and I certainly did not construct the differences that were apparent to all.

Given that race realism is the default, common-sense position, proponents of social constructivism need to offer arguments for their claim. In this essay, I criticize four arguments for the social construction of race, which I characterize as follows: (1) the argument from the social construction of knowledge in general; (2) the argument from changing racial classifications; (3) the argument from continua; and (4) the argument from the silence of science. This is not an exhaustive list, nor is this a "scholarly" survey and critique.[2] I chose these arguments simply because they are commonly used in middle-brow online debates. I conclude by treating the thesis of the social construction of race as a social construct itself, exposing the political agenda and power relations behind social constructivism.

1. THE SOCIAL CONSTRUCTION OF KNOWLEDGE IN GENERAL

One argument for the social construction of race is a simple deduction from the general thesis that "All knowledge is socially constructed." This is a philosophical thesis about the relationship between mind and reality, which holds that there is no single correct account of

---

[2] For a more comprehensive survey of the case for race realism and against social constructivism, see Richard McCulloch, "Race: Reality and Denial," *The Occidental Quarterly*, vol. 2, no. 4 (Winter 2002–2003): 5–26.

any aspect of reality, but rather a plurality of equally valid accounts which are relative to the contingent circumstances of different communities. For instance, there is the scientific account of the origin of the species, and there is the Biblical account, both of which are products of different communities, and there is no neutral standpoint or criterion that allows us to claim that one approach is better or truer than another.

I believe that this sort of relativism is philosophically incoherent in itself.[3] But it also fails as a justification of the social construction of race because, in a sense, it proves too much. For if everything is a social construct, the concept loses all utility. Social construction only makes sense if there is a contrast term, namely objective natural facts.

But if everything is a social construct, then we have to ask: Is the social construct *race* more like the social construct *money* or the social construct *gravity*? Because it is in society's power to change money, but it is not in our power to change gravity. A philosopher who defends the idea that gravity is a social construct still leaves the lecture hall by the door rather than the window because he knows that one ignores some social constructs at one's own risk.

The social constructivist clearly wants race to be like money rather than gravity, but if everything is a social construct, he needs to offer an additional argument to prove that racial inequalities can be abolished by social fiat.

2. Changing Racial Classifications

One of the most common arguments for the social construction of race is along the following lines: (1) If ra-

---

[3] See Paul Boghossian, *Fear of Knowledge: Against Relativism and Constructivism* (Oxford: Clarendon, 2007).

cial differences are real, then racial classification schemes will not vary from time to time and place to place. (2) Racial classification schemes vary from time to time and place to place. For instance, the same mixed-race individual might be considered black or white in different places and at different times.[4] Therefore, racial differences are not real. And, since racial differences are either real or social constructs, they must be social constructs.

This argument has two main problems.

The first premise is simply false because it elides the distinction between reality and opinion. Racial differences can be perfectly real, but people's *opinions* about racial differences can vary widely. Since human beings are fallible, there can be many opinions about one and the same fact. But that does not make the facts any less objective. It just proves that people frequently fail to be as objective as the facts.

The oft-cited example of varying standards of blackness proves nothing about racial realities. First, the very idea of categorizing mixed-race individuals as black or white is problematic, simply because they are mixed. Given that they are neither black nor white, it is not surprising that people make different decisions if they have to classify them as one or the other. Thus it may be arbitrary social convention to say that Barack Obama is a black man. But it is an objective fact of nature that he had a white mother and a black father and is therefore half white and half black.

3. CUTTING THE CONTINUUM

Another common argument for the social construction of race, and of knowledge in general, depends on the distinction between differences of *degree* and differences

---

[4] Ta-Nehisi Coates, "What We Mean When We Say 'Race Is a Social Construct,'" *The Atlantic*, May 15, 2013.

of *kind*, and runs as follows. (1) If racial differences are real differences of kind, then there should not be a continuum of intermediate types. (2) There are continuua of intermediate types between races. Therefore, there is only one human race, and distinctions between races are not found in nature but constructed by human beings. We carve up the continuum. Nature does not come separated into different kinds.[5]

There are two major problems with this argument.

The first premise strikes me as highly dubious: Just because there are continua in nature does not mean that there are no real distinctions between parts of a given continuum. In terms of color, red may shade off into orange, and different cultures might have different words for colors and make finer or grosser distinctions between them. But does this mean that there are no real, observable differences between, say, red and blue?

Evolutionary theory posits the common origin and evolutionary continuity of all life on earth. Does that continuity mean, therefore, that there are no real differences between mammals and birds, or birds and reptiles,

---

[5] An underlying assumption of this argument is that to truly know objective reality, the mind must be passive and reality must simply inscribe itself upon it. Thus if the mind is in any way active in the process of gaining knowledge, we no longer know objective reality but only human constructs. Ayn Rand offers a *reductio ad absurdum* of this argument, although she mistakenly applies it to Kant: "[Kant's] argument, in essence, ran as follows: man is *limited* to a consciousness of a specific nature, which perceives by specific means and no others, therefore, his consciousness is not valid; man is blind, because he has eyes — deaf, because he has ears — deluded, because he has a mind — and the things he perceives do not exist, *because* he perceives them" Ayn Rand, "For the New Intellectual," in *For the New Intellectual: The Philosophy of Ayn Rand* (New York: Random House, 1961), p. 33.

or nematodes and human beings? Is the difference between dinosaurs and humans merely a "social construct"? Did dinosaurs not exist before human beings were around to "socially construct" them?

If race is a social construct, is the human race as a whole a "social construct" too? What then is society? What is society made up of *before* the social construction of the human race? Is society also a social construct, which would seem to get us into an infinite regress (society is a social construct of a social construct of a social construct . . .)? Or is society not a social construct? Is it just a fact of nature? Is it just *here*? Then why can't other things be facts of nature, like human beings and dinosaurs?

The second premise is also problematic. Anthropologists claim that all human races descend from common ancestors. But at different points in time, the five distinct human races—Caucasoid, Mongoloid, Congoid, Capoid, and Australoid—branched off and differentiated themselves from both their common ancestors and one another. After developing in isolation for enough time to attain distinctive traits, these races then came into contact with one another and gave rise to mixed populations.[6] But the existence of racially mixed individuals no more overthrows the real distinction between races than the existence of green paint refutes the existence of blue and yellow paint.[7]

4. THE SILENCE OF SCIENCE

Another common claim of the social constructivists is that science does not give adequate support to the idea of real racial distinctions, thus social constructivism is

---

[6] For an accessible account of racial evolution that remains valid today, see Carleton S. Coon, *The Origin of Races* (New York: Knopf, 1962). See also Coon's *The Living Races of Man*.

[7] John R. Baker makes this point in his *Race* (New York: Oxford University Press, 1974), p. 100.

true. The argument runs as follows. (1) If there are real racial differences, then science will explain them. (2) Science has not explained racial differences. Therefore, there are no real racial differences. Since racial differences are either real or socially constructed, race is a social construct.

This argument has four grave problems.

First, race realism is based on observed racial differences, not on scientific theories of race. Human beings perceived racial differences long before the emergence of science, and we perceive them still, even those of us who are entirely innocent of racial science (as most social constructivists happen to be). Thus the first premise is simply false: The *reality* of race does not depend on the success or failure of scientific *theories* of race. Theories may rise and fall, but observable differences remain.

As for the second premise: Scientists would beg to differ.[8] We can determine the race of an individual from the morpoholgical or genetic analysis of a single bone or strand of hair.

Of course, the social constructivists are not exactly clear about what constitutes the failure of science to explain race, but they generally insinuate that science has either (1) failed to come up with a single differentiating trait possessed by all members of a race and not possessed by other races,[9] or (2) that no such theory has attained universal acceptance.

But the demand for a single essential differentiating trait for each race is arbitrary. Nature does not have to

---

[8] For a simple and compelling summary of the science of race, see J. Philippe Rushton, *Race, Evolution, and Behavior: A Life History Perspective*, 2nd special abridged edition (Port Huron, Michigan: Charles Darwin Research Institute, 2000).

[9] See Joseph L. Graves, Jr., "The Biological Case against Race," *American Outlook*, Spring 2002, p. 31.

conform to our demands. And the fact that a theory does not attain universal acceptance has nothing to do with its truth, given the variability and fallibility of human opinions. Frankly, I believe that most social constructivists are intellectually dishonest. Thus no theory of objective racial differences will ever gain universal assent, no matter how well founded it may be.

Another problem with this argument is that it overlooks the fact that science is a process that unfolds over time. Thus even if the second premise were true, the conclusion does not follow, simply because science might not have come up with the correct account *just yet*. But wait.

A final problem with this argument is its assumption that in the absence of a scientific explanation of race, the only alternative is social constructivism. In fact, the default position is race realism based on empirical observation, which does not depend upon scientific explanation at all.

SOCIAL CONSTRUCTIVISM AS SOCIAL CONSTRUCT

Social constructivists typically do not limit their thesis to race. Many claim that all knowledge is a social construct, or even that reality itself is a social construct. Thus it is fair to ask: Is social constructivism itself a social construct? If social constructivism is a social construct, this has three important implications:

1. Like all social constructs, social constructivism is the product of a unique set of historically contingent circumstances.
2. Since every society is divided into the rulers and the ruled, every social construct will be marked by the agenda of those who hold power.
3. If social constructivism is a social construct, not a natural fact, its acceptance or rejection is

> not based on reason and nature but on social
> incentives: moral and political commitment
> for the true believers—brainwashing, greed,
> and fear for the rest.

Social constructivism has a long philosophical pedigree, but today it functions as the metaphysical postulate of egalitarian social engineering projects to equalize the races by revolutionizing European-defined and dominated societies. Of course, this revolution cannot produce racial equality, but it can create a new racial hierarchy in which Europeans are subordinate. Social constructivism thus serves the interests of a new emerging social elite, an alliance of rootless plutocrats, non-whites, sexual minorities, and other outsiders, in which the organized Jewish community is the senior and guiding partner. Thus social constructivism is an element of what Kevin MacDonald calls the "culture of critique": the critique and overthrow of European civilization by Jewish-inspired and dominated intellectual movements like Marxism, psychoanalysis, the Frankfurt School, feminism, deconstructionism, and most forms of postmodernism.[10]

These movements are characterized by pseudo-science, obscurantism, and crass ethno-political advocacy. They acquired their influence not through reason and science but through the subversion of the educational, cultural, and political institutions of European societies. They perpetuate their influence though the indoctrination of the impressionable and the suppression of dissent.

Thus social constructivism cannot be defeated merely

---

[10] Kevin MacDonald, *The Culture of Critique: An Evolutionary Analysis of Jewish Involvement in Twentieth-Century Intellectual and Political Movements* (Westport, Conn.: Praeger, 1998).

by criticizing its astonishingly poor arguments, which in large part are merely tools of self-conscious and cynical deception. If you lop off one argument, the hydra just sprouts another.

Instead, social constructivism must be defeated on its own terms: by altering the social conditions that give rise to it; by changing who rules this society; by disempowering and silencing its advocates just as they disempower and silence their critics. In short, social constructivism must be socially deconstructed and replaced by a new cultural and political hegemony that is aligned with reason, reality, and white interests. And we can do that in good conscience, because social constructivism is a false and pernicious ideology, nothing more.

Race realism is the default position of common sense. It is, moreover, supported by the best biological science. There is no good case for the social construction of race. It would be truer to say that society is a racial construct, meaning that society is the creation of human beings, who exist as part of nature and whose biological traits shape and constrain society and culture.

But once society is established, social conventions shape the underlying race by instituting eugenic and dysgenic breeding incentives or simply by legislating the extermination of entire groups. Nature comes before culture, but once culture exists, it turns back on and modifies nature.[11] Only in this specific sense can one say that race is a (partial) social "construct," although it would be better to drop the misleading language of construction altogether.

---

[11] For a recent and compelling account of genetic and cultural co-evolution, see Gregory Cochran and Henry Harpending, *The 10,000 Year Explosion: How Civilization Accelerated Human Evolution* (New York: Basic Books, 2009).

SPEND YOURSELF,
SAVE THE WORLD

Sometime in 2003, I was feeling tired and thinking of knocking off work on a movement-related project. It was 2:30 a.m., and I had not been sleeping well for a while. But then a question occurred to me: "What are you saving yourself for?" Did I really need my beauty sleep? Everything we save has to be spent eventually, because death will take it away in the end. And we will not save the world by saving ourselves. We will save it only by spending ourselves.

So I put in another 90 minutes, then slept soundly and got up the next day with renewed energy and eagerness. For I discovered that sometimes when we ask more of ourselves, we find that we have more to give—more than we ever suspected.

A perennial question debated by American Rightists is why politics continually drifts to the Left.[1] An important factor is simply that the Left is morally stronger than the Right,[2] which gives them a systematic advantage.

Moral strength has two dimensions.

First, Leftists are on average more dedicated, idealistic, and altruistic than Rightists. Meaning that they are willing to work harder and sacrifice more to bring about their ideals.

Second, Leftists and mainstream Rightists both share the same basic egalitarian individualist outlook, but Leftists are truer to their ideals, whereas Rightists are more

---

[1] See my "Metapolitics and Occult Warfare," in *New Right vs. Old Right.*

[2] See my "Learning from the Left," in *New Right vs. Old Right.*

willing to compromise their ideals out of timidity, greed, and inertia. But other things being equal, a principled man is morally stronger than a hypocrite, so the Leftists always wrangle the Right around in the end.

Many racial nationalists reject egalitarian individualism. We think that individualism and equality are not entirely without value. But they are not the highest values of a society. The highest value is the common good: the preservation and flourishing of our people. When equality or individualism conflict with that, the common good must always win out.

But although we reject the moral premises of the Left, destroying one of their moral advantages at the root, we have not yet equaled the Left's other moral advantage: their superior idealism, commitment, and self-sacrifice. And other things being equal, the team that can muster these to a greater degree will win.

In this area, the main stumbling block of the Right is bourgeois morality. As I define it, the bourgeois ethic holds that the highest good is a long, comfortable, secure life. This is in contradistinction to the aristocratic ethos that holds honor as the highest value, to which the aristocrat is willing to sacrifice both his life and his wealth. (Bourgeois man, by contrast, is all too willing to sacrifice his honor to pursue wealth and extend his life.) The bourgeois ethic is also opposed to the willingness of idealists to die for principles, whether religious, political, or philosophical.

The bourgeois ethos was articulated by early modern philosophers like Hobbes, Locke, and Hume, who heap scorn on the "pride and vainglory" of aristocrats and the "superstition and enthusiasm" of fanatics, for these values make men "contentious and quarrelsome," which interferes with the peaceful pursuit of happiness by the "industrious and rational."

In terms of Plato's tripartition of the soul between

reason, spirit (*thumos*), and desire, the fanatic is ruled by reason since his highest values are matters of principle; the aristocrat is ruled by spirit since his highest value is honor; and the bourgeois man is ruled by desire, since his highest value is a long, peaceful, and prosperous life.

The bourgeois pursuit of happiness basically reduces human motives to greed and fear: greed for more life, more property, more security—and fear of death, insecurity, and material loss. Over time, the very possibility of other motives—idealism and self-sacrifice—have receded from the bourgeois understanding of psychology.

That pretty much sums up the mentality of American bourgeois conservatives, whose entire ethic is devoted to saving themselves and accumulating wealth rather than expending them on higher values. When he encounters people with higher concerns, bourgeois man either argues that they are merely acting out of a disguised form of egoism, or, when this fails, he clucks disapprovingly about the inscrutable wellsprings and evil consequences of human fanaticism.

The Left mobilizes greater dedication, idealism, and self-sacrifice than the Right simply because it disdains bourgeois man's selfishness and anti-intellectualism. Even Marxism, which has an entirely materialistic value system, in effect "backs into" idealism and self-sacrifice merely by negating the bourgeois ethos. White Nationalism desperately needs to do the same.

Unfortunately, the American White Nationalist movement is thoroughly bourgeois. We have a culture of excuse-making and failure, a "can't do" attitude. I have sat through far too many meetings in which weary old sell-outs persuade young idealists to follow the bourgeois path: keep their heads down, keep their mouths shut, pursue their careers, and accumulate money, until . . .

Well, that is never made clear. But the answer is: (1) until they die with their fortunes and mainstream reputations intact, without accomplishing a fraction of what they could have done with a different ethic, or (2) until men who don't take such advice create a movement worth following.

The European movement is far healthier than the North American one, primarily because the United States and Canada are entirely bourgeois societies, whereas Europe still has remnants of a pre-bourgeois ethos. North America was largely peopled by those who preferred the pursuit of economic opportunities over ties to their homeland, whereas those who remained behind faced the same choice and elected to stay. Such preferences continue to matter today.

Even American White Nationalists who reject conservatism still think in entirely bourgeois psychological terms and cannot fathom motives other than greed and fear. But we can't beat our enemies if we can't understand them or ourselves.

There are White Nationalists who deny that morality plays any role in politics at all, since people are entirely motivated by greed and fear. They are unaware that this concept of human motivation is itself a moral code, namely the bourgeois one, and that there are other moral codes that disdain such mean motives.

There are White Nationalists who claim that altruism or idealism are merely masks for purely selfish motives. But they do not explain why, if everyone is really just selfish, so many people bother faking a morality that they claim is practiced by nobody at all.

In biological terms, altruism is any act that decreases the fitness of the actor while increasing the fitness of related individuals, which also helps promote the actor's own genes in those whom he benefits. Parasitism is when an actor works to benefit genetically unrelated individuals, such as when a bird incubates the eggs and feeds the chicks of a brood parasite species.

White dispossession, including white self-destruction or racial suicide, is taking place because our biological altruism has been transformed into biological parasitism. Regardless of who is promoting and benefiting from such behavior, it would not have been possible if whites did not have a predisposition to moral universalism and impartiality, which makes it possible for us to conceive of even dramatically unrelated people as members of a common moral community. It would also not be possible if our sense of high-mindedness did not include a willingness to make moral gestures toward strangers—even at the risk they will not be reciprocated—in the hope of expanding our moral community, and to persist in these gestures again and again, even when they are rebuffed or exploited. A crucial task of White Nationalists is to combat such self-destructive moralism, and to scale our altruism back within biologically functional bounds.

But if the Left is too altruistic, the bourgeois Right is not altruistic enough. Prizing one's individual life above the race is a silly thing. Higher values are objective and persistent, not subjective and fleeting. The individual dies, but the race can live on—if it finds the right defenders. Bourgeois individualists tend to lose sight of the purpose of wealth and reputation, which only make a difference if spent, not saved, and are wasted if death takes them intact.

As a movement, we need to cultivate idealists who take principles seriously and warriors who are willing to fight and, if necessary, die for our people. Only these people have the moral strength to begin pulling the political spectrum back towards the Right.

Our impact on the world is based on what we spend, not what we save. We have to spend ourselves to save the world.

IN MY GRANDIOSE MOMENTS . . .

Once a reader asked me, ever so gently, if I did not think my fundraising goals to be a bit grandiose. My answer was simple: Compared to our ultimate goals, no, they don't seem grandiose at all . . .

There is a poetic moment in Paul Verhoeven's *Starship Troopers* when Johnny Rico, who has just washed out of the Mobile Infantry, is leaving base. Suddenly, he sees people on the parade ground breaking formation and running. And, perhaps out of curiosity, perhaps out of a kind of herding or schooling instinct, he starts running along with them. "War! We're going to war!" one of his former comrades shouts.

The scene beautifully communicates the feeling of being caught up in events, of being a tiny piece of driftwood carried along by the great surge of history. Of course, this is not something that only happens in times of war. Indeed, it happens all the time. It is like gravity, like the air we breathe. It is child's play to put bubble-headed aliens on screen. It takes a masterful filmmaker to make us experience and wonder at what is utterly close and commonplace.

All of us, all the time, are subjected to historical forces we cannot control. We are objects, not agents. Things are done *to* us, not *by* us. Most of our actions are piddling, reactive, and entirely ineffectual—at least if we try to go against the current. Somebody else establishes the pace, and we try to catch up. Somebody else sinks the ship, and we try to tread water. Somebody else tanks the economy, and we end up bailing them out. Somebody else opened the borders, and we just have to cope with the depressed wages and increased crime, corruption, ugliness, and alienation. That's life—for most people, most of the time.

But there are people who exercise power and bear responsibility. The system does not just run itself. What would it be like to be a historical agent, not just one of their pawns? What would it be like to be the master of one's own destiny, rather than a plaything of the powerful? What would it be like to live in a system that advances our individual and group interests rather than subordinates and sacrifices them? What would be like to belong to a people that has a sense of destiny—and is in control of how that destiny unfolds?

The purpose of White Nationalism is for whites to regain control of our destiny as a race, to make us collectively masters of our own fate. We are not egalitarians. We are not individualists. We understand that our powers and responsibilities differ. We understand that not everyone can exercise agency all the time. But our goal is to create a system in which the few govern in the interests of all, in which the limited agency of each individual is amplified rather than smothered by the social order.

It seems like a tall order. But such systems are not utopias. We know they are possible, because they have been actual. They have existed in history. They even exist in the present day in the Far East. We can, of course, improve upon them. But the blueprints already exist. The real question is: How do we get there from here? A related question is: How can one experience, in the present day, the world we are trying to create in the future? Because some of us will never live to see the Promised Land.

Both questions have the same answer: By acting to bring about a White Nationalist society, by participating in the White Nationalist cause in whatever way possible, to whatever extent possible, we can create an ideal world and have a taste of it in the present day.

I am fond of the phrase that those who fight for the Golden Age live in it today. I do not mean this in a merely symbolic sense. It is a very real phenomenon: The world we are fighting for is one in which whites are masters of our fate, in which we have control of our destiny, in which we are agents not objects of history. Acting to create that world *is* taking control of your own destiny and working for the freedom of our people. Each white who moves from being a passive spectator to being an active agent of our cause brings us one step closer to victory. Working to create a White Nationalist society is to participate in some way in the society we wish to create.

But what is to be done?

Counter-Currents has always stood for pluralism. There is not "one right way" to do this. I have consistently argued that our movement will function best if we (1) try new approaches, (2) seek to tailor our message to every different white constituency, and (3) allow each individual to determine his own level of explicitness and involvement.

But, by the same token, I am always encouraging people to become *more explicit* and *more involved*, to get people outside their comfort zones, to become more radical, and not just in the sense of understanding things to their roots, but in the sense of being increasingly active, committed, and fanatical.

The best thing is to be an explicit White Nationalist. We need a lot more of them.[1]

The next best thing is to be a secret agent, working actively within the system to undermine it.[2]

The next best thing after that is to actively support those who are willing to do more than you.

---

[1] See "Explicit White Nationalism" in *New Right vs. Old Right*.

[2] See "Secret Agents" in *New Right vs. Old Right*.

If you are not willing to do any of those things, then please, at least do no harm.[3]

But, for the love of everything good and beautiful in this world, *you have to stop being passive consumers of free information on the internet, or mere kibitzers on online forums.* That was the beginning for most of us, but it is only the beginning, and if it is the end of your involvement, then our race is going to die.

One of the secrets of Communism is that it mobilized enormous energy and dedication from people because its goals demanded them.[4] They promised themselves the world, and they went about delivering it.

Although manic grandiosity and malignant narcissism are the two more destructive personality disorders in our circles, we have to risk grandiosity. We have to put aside our humility, put aside our modesty, and entertain the possibility that *we can become world-historical individuals*: that we can change the course of history, that we can save our race, that we can turn it from the path to extinction and return it to the path of godhood.

And it is not just about saving the white race. It is about saving *all life on earth*—the only life in the cosmos as far as we know—because if our enemies win, this blue planet will someday be reduced to a dead cinder in space. You can save all the other endangered species by saving the most important one, our own.

Yes, this cause is *that important*, and by moving our cause forward, you share in that importance. If your life lacks meaning and purpose, this is where you find them.

There have been times when I wished that I had never gotten involved with White Nationalism. I tend to focus on the negative and forget about the positive. Sometimes I brood over the fact that the craziest, crookedest, most

---

[3] See "'First, Do No Harm'" in *New Right vs. Old Right*.

[4] See "Learning from the Left" in *New Right vs. Old Right*.

loathsome people I have ever encountered have been White Nationalists—forgetting that the finest people I know are White Nationalists as well.

My complaining finally angered a good friend, a secret agent who does as much as he can for the cause. He told me that I lead an enviable life, that I work full time for the most important cause in the cosmos, that I can speak the truth as I see it for the rest of my days. Then he reminded me of the basic premise of *Buffy the Vampire Slayer*: Buffy has super-powers and is part of a secret initiatic society doing battle with the forces of evil. Night after night, she is literally saving the world. And yet . . . all she wants to be is an ordinary high school cheerleader.

Well, when you put it that way, I choose to fight evil and save the world. Allow yourself a grandiose moment, and then choose to join us.

IT'S OKAY TO BE
WHITE

The Left characterizes the United States and other white countries around the world as systems of "white supremacy" and "white privilege."

White Nationalists claim that the United States and most other white countries are committed to "white genocide": the "great replacement" of whites by nonwhites, which is the predictable consequence of political decisions to promote sub-replacement white fertility, race-mixing, and race-replacement immigration.

Which of these diametrically opposed positions is true?

There's an easy way to find out. In a white supremacist society, you should be able to declare that "It's okay to be white" without controversy or consequences.

Indeed, in a white supremacist society, the only criticism you might receive is for being too tepid. After all, "okay" simply means "adequate but not especially good." It is the equivalent to giving white existence a grade of "C." Being white is apparently nothing to envy, but you wouldn't kill yourself over it either.

When the slogan "It's okay to be white" first appeared on 4chan's /pol/ in 2017, it was promoted as a diagnostic tool to help convince "normies" that we live under anti-white regimes. After all, how could anyone object to "It's okay to be white"?

The slogan does not claim that being white is *great*. It does not claim that being white is *better*. It merely says that being white is *okay*, which is the faintest possible praise. Furthermore, "It's okay to be white" says nothing at all about other races. It certainly doesn't denigrate them.

So on what grounds could one object to saying "It's okay to be white"? As Tucker Carlson put it, "What's the correct position? That it's not okay to be white?"

If multiculturalism is truly an ideology of equality and inclusion, then multiculturalists should have no problem saying "It's okay to be white." They would grant it the same status as "Black is beautiful" and "It's okay to be different." Indeed, whiteness is one form of difference.

Clearly, one could object to a statement as innocuous as "It's okay to be white" *only if one really has something against white people,* specifically a deep hatred or prejudice. This is why it is such a useful diagnostic tool.

"It's okay to be white" flyers and stickers were posted widely in the United States and other white countries, primarily in the Anglosphere. As its creators predicted, the slogan provoked an immediate and intense backlash, far out of proportion to the inoffensive message.

Upon seeing "It's okay to be white" signs and stickers, the first reaction of hundreds of people was to call the police. This can be verified simply by entering the words "police" and "It's okay to be white" in the search engine of your choice. (DuckDuckGo gives the best results.) This happened even in the United States, where the First Amendment to the US Constitution protects freedom of speech. Here are a couple of my favorite headlines:

❖ "Sickening to Know People Think Like This"—
   Police Investigate "It's Okay to Be White" Signs
   in Scotland
❖ 150+ Cases of Outrage, Manhunts over "It's OK
   to be White," Poster Activist Responds

Indeed, sometimes people deemed these posters too hot for the local cops to handle, so the Federal Bureau of Investigation was called in:

❖ FBI probes signs defending white privilege
   found at Vermont universities

To put this in context, ask yourself how many flyers and stickers you see in a typical day. Dozens? On a university campus, you might see hundreds. Then ask yourself how many times you were tempted to call the police. Most people would have to answer: never. But when hundreds of people saw "It's okay to be white," they were convinced that it is illegal—or that it should be.

Once the police were called, of course the press were alerted, and locals were asked to share their opinions about the flyers. Most people interviewed are certain that "It's okay to be white" constitutes "hate speech," even though it says nothing negative or hateful about anyone.

I'll pull quotes from the first article listed above to give a sense of the sort of statements that are typical: John Swinney, Deputy First Minister of the Scottish Government, declared: "This is atrocious and has no place in Perth or any other part of our country. We must stand together to resist this unacceptable material." Peter Barrett, a Perth councilor, said: "This is despicable hate speech. It is covert racism disguising white supremacist views. People should be in no doubt this is no innocuous joke." Local antiracists claimed that people of color had called to share their feelings. The "terrifying attitudes" expressed by "It's okay to be white" made them feel "sickened," "disgusted," and "unsafe."

My favorite political statement comes from Mayor William Dickinson, Jr. of Wallingford, Connecticut: "whoever posted the signs reading 'It's okay to be white' don't speak for the people of Wallingford," he declared, speaking for the people of Wallingford.

Given that higher education is a citadel of the extreme Left throughout the white world, reactions to "It's okay to be white" on university campuses are especially extreme, as one can see by typing the phrase plus the word "campus" into any search engine. Here are my favorite headlines:

❖ "It's OK to Be White" Flyers Lead to Promise of "Severest Disciplinary Action" by Western Conn. State U.
❖ Ohio universities involve FBI in investigation of "It's okay to be white" and white nationalist group's postings on campus
❖ Oklahoma law school student is questioned by FBI Joint Terrorism Task Force and expelled for posting "It's Okay to be White" flyers on campus

Naturally, university administrators—especially in Podunk schools—can be counted on for the most vehement denunciations of "It's okay to be white." The fulminations of President John Clark of Western Connecticut State University are typical: "I want to state directly and without equivocation that if any member of our university community is found to be party to these revolting actions they will be subject to the severest disciplinary actions, including dismissal as well as possible civil and criminal actions." These are not empty threats. A student at Oklahoma City University School of Law was expelled for posting "It's okay to be white" and ended up talking to the FBI's Joint Terrorism Task Force.

My favorite "It's okay to be white" story is from Australia (75% white), where Senator Pauline Hanson of the nationalist One Nation Party proposed a non-binding statement condemning anti-white racism and declaring "It's okay to be white." Although politicians constantly append their names to all manner of high-minded but empty proclamations, and although not a single Senator in Australia should have had a problem with affirming that "It's okay to be white," the resolution was narrowly defeated on October 15, 2018.

Is any of this behavior consistent with the claim that the United States and other white countries are systems of "white supremacism" and "white privilege"? Obviously not. If we lived in a white supremacist system, people would be *afraid* to call the police about "It's okay to be white" flyers and stickers. College administrators would be *afraid* to threaten students with punishment. Legislators would be *afraid* to vote against "It's okay to be white." But instead, they know that the entire establishment—political, business, media, and academic—is anti-white. Thus it will reward their behavior with an approving pat on the head.

But just how anti-white is this system? Is it really committed to white genocide? One can interpret "It's okay to be white" in at least two ways. The most natural reading is "It's *good* to be white." But the word "okay" is such tepid praise that maybe we should interpret the phrase more along these lines: "It is *acceptable* to be white," or better, "It is acceptable for white people to be, i.e., to exist," or "Don't kill yourself over being white."

A society in which one can be punished for merely asserting that "It is acceptable for white people to exist" is obviously hostile to the very existence of whites. It is a society in which it is *unacceptable* for white people to exist. But if this is true, wouldn't it be natural to explore ways of getting rid of whites altogether? The genocidal implications are obvious.

One might counter that those who object to "It's okay to be white" do not object to the *existence* of white people but merely to *white pride* and *white self-assertion*. Of course, "It's okay to be white" is not a statement of pride and self-assertion. It is absurdly unassuming, almost an apology for existing. But even that is apparently too much self-worth for the preachers of "white guilt" and self-abnegation.

However, even the ideology of "white guilt" is implicitly genocidal. First of all, there is no path to absolution from white guilt. As long as non-whites are unequal to whites, whites will somehow be held guilty. And because inequality is natural, it will always exist. Second, we live in a world of racial strife, in which a race without pride or self-assertiveness—a race burdened with eternal guilt and self-reproach—will fall prey to races without such handicaps.

The best-case scenario is that whites will forever be poisoned with spurious guilt for the inadequacies of others, then milked for free stuff. In short: slavery. The worst-case scenario is outright genocide. And given that violence and instability increase with diversity, orderly factory-farm slavery is the least likely outcome. Thus objecting to white pride—or even mere white "okayness"—is ultimately objecting to white existence as such.

Do the people who object to "It's okay to be white" *consciously* promote white genocide, or do they "know not what they do"? Most of them don't know what they are doing. White genocide is the long-term result of the principles they act on, but most people don't think about the long-term. They unwittingly promote white genocide while thinking they are being moral, pragmatic, or even selfish, because they know that they will be rewarded for anti-white signaling.

The great value of "It's okay to be white" is that when one attacks such banal pro-white sentiments, it brings the implicitly genocidal programing of the Left very close to the surface. If you get hysterical about white people merely existing and not feeling suicidal about it, what do you really stand for anyway?

Of course, the real point of "It's okay to be white" is not to save the souls of anti-whites but to educate ordinary people. This is why we need to keep "It's okay to be white" constantly in the news. The same is true with "All Lives Matter," although "White Lives Matter" is more to the point.

Force the Left to say "It's *not* okay to be white." Force

them to say "White lives *don't* matter." And make sure that everyone knows it.

Also, be sure to take down names. If a doctor, lawyer, professor, or politician does not think it is okay to be white, then how can he be trusted to serve the interests of whites? White racists are routinely fired on the assumption that they cannot deal professionally with non-whites. Anti-white racists need to be held to the same standard. A white person would have to be nuts to go under the knife of a surgeon who says "White lives don't matter." We would be foolish to expect anti-white professors to grade us justly. Whites must be protected from such people. It is our job to hold institutions accountable.

When the entire establishment comes together to denounce "It's okay to be white" or "White lives matter," it decisively refutes the Left's thesis that we live in systems of white supremacism and privilege. It also exposes that multiculturalism does not envision a world in which whites enjoy equality and harmony with other groups.

The multiculturalist utopia does not envision whites at all.

RECOMMENDED READING

Patrick J. Buchanan, *The Death of the West: How Dying Populations & Immigrant Invasions Imperil Our Culture & Civilization* (New York: St. Martin's Press, 2001).

_____, *Suicide of a Superpower: Will America Survive to 2025?* (New York: Thomas Dunne Books, 2011).

Ricardo Duchesne, *The Uniqueness of Western Civilization* (Leiden, Netherlands: E. J. Brill, 2011).

Guillaume Faye, *Why We Fight: Manifesto of the European Resistance*, trans. Michael O'Meara (London: Arktos, 2011).

Samuel Francis, *Essential Writings on Race*, ed. Jared Taylor (Oakton, Va.: New Century Foundation, 2007).

Gregory Hood, *Waking Up from the American Dream* (San Francisco: Counter-Currents, 2016).

Greg Johnson, *Confessions of a Reluctant Hater*, second, expanded ed. (San Francisco: Counter-Currents, 2016).

_____, *In Defense of Prejudice* (San Francisco: Counter-Currents, 2016).

_____, *New Right vs. Old Right* (San Francisco: Counter-Currents, 2013).

_____, *Toward a New Nationalism* (San Francisco: Counter-Currents, 2019).

_____, *Truth, Justice, & a Nice White Country* (San Francisco: Counter-Currents, 2015).

_____, *You Asked for It: Selected Interviews*, vol. 1 (San Francisco: Counter-Currents, 2017).

Greg Johnson, ed., *North American New Right*, vol. 1 (San Francisco: Counter-Currents, 2012).

_____, *North American New Right*, vol. 2 (San Francisco: Counter-Currents, 2017).

_____, *The Alternative Right* (San Francisco: Counter-Currents, 2018).

Michael Levin, *Why Race Matters* (Oakton, Va.: New Century Books, 2016).

Richard Lynn, *The Global Bell Curve: Race, IQ, & Inequality Worldwide* (Augusta, Ga.: Washington Summit Publishers, 2008).

Kevin MacDonald, *Cultural Insurrections: Essays on Jewish Influence, Anti-Semitism, & Western Civilization* (Atlanta: The Occidental Press, 2007).

_____, *The Culture of Critique: An Evolutionary Analysis of Jewish Involvement in Twentieth-Century Intellectual & Political Movements*, revised edition (Bloomington, Ind., 1st Books, 2002).

Steven Pinker, *The Blank Slate: The Modern Denial of Human Nature* (New York: Penguin, 2003).

Robert Putnam, *Bowling Alone: The Collapse & Revival of American Community* (New York: Simon & Schuster, 2001).

Wilmot Robertson, *The Dispossessed Majority*, fourth edition (Cape Canaveral, Fl.: Howard Allen, 1981).

_____, *The Ethnostate: An Unblinkered Prospectus for an Advanced Statecraft* (Cape Canaveral, Fl.: Howard Allen, 1992).

J. Philippe Rushton, *Race, Evolution, & Behavior: A Life History Perspective*, third unabridged edition (Port Huron, Michigan: Charles Darwin Research Institute, 2000).

Frank Salter, *On Genetic Interests: Family, Ethnicity, & Humanity in an Age of Mass Migration* (New Brunswick, N.J.: Transaction Publishers, 2006).

Jared Taylor, *If We Do Nothing: Essays & Reviews from 25 Years of White Advocacy* (Oakton, Va.: New Century Books, 2016).

_____, *White Identity: Racial Consciousness in the 21st Century* (Oakton, Va.: New Century Books, 2011).

INDEX

ABOUT THE AUTHOR

Greg Johnson, Ph.D. is Editor-in-Chief of Counter-Currents Publishing Ltd., as well as Editor of *North American New Right,* its webzine (http://www.counter-currents.com/) and occasional print journal.

He is the author of *Confessions of a Reluctant Hater* (San Francisco: Counter-Currents, 2010; second, expanded ed., 2016); *New Right vs. Old Right* (Counter-Currents, 2013); *Truth, Justice, & a Nice White Country* (Counter-Currents, 2015); *In Defense of Prejudice* (Counter-Currents, 2017); *You Asked for It: Selected Interviews,* vol. 1 (Counter-Currents, 2017); *The White Nationalist Manifesto* (Counter-Currents, 2018); *Toward a New Nationalism* (Counter-Currents, 2019); and *From Plato to Postmodernism* (Counter-Currents, 2019).

Under the pen name Trevor Lynch, he is the author of *Trevor Lynch's White Nationalist Guide to the Movies* (Counter-Currents, 2012), *Son of Trevor Lynch's White Nationalist Guide to the Movies* (Counter-Currents, 2015), and *Return of the Son of Trevor Lynch's CENSORED Guide to the Movies* (Counter-Currents, 2019).

He has also edited many books, including *North American New Right,* vol. 1 (Counter-Currents, 2012); *North American New Right,* vol. 2 (Counter-Currents, 2017); *Dark Right: Batman Viewed from the Right* (with Gregory Hood) (Counter-Currents, 2018); and *The Alternative Right* (Counter-Currents, 2018).

His writings have been translated into Czech, Danish, Dutch, Estonian, French, German, Greek, Hungarian, Norwegian, Polish, Portuguese, Russian, Slovak, Spanish, Swedish, and Ukrainian.